# Managing Presidential Objectives

### RICHARD ROSE

First published in the USA 1976
First published in the United Kingdom 1977

Published by

THE MACMILLAN PRESS LTD

*London and Basingstoke*
*Associated companies in New York*
*Dublin Melbourne Johannesburg and Madras*

ISBN 0 333 21748 9

*Printed in Great Britain by*
UNWIN BROTHERS LTD
*Old Woking, Surrey*

*This book is sold subject*
*to the standard conditions*
*of the Net Book Agreement*

# Managing Presidential
# Objectives

*I was to learn later in life that we tend to meet any new situation by reorganizing, and a wonderful method it can be for creating the illusion of progress while producing confusion, inefficiency and demoralization.*

Gaius Petronius

To Those Who Serve the Great Republic

# Contents

# A List of Tables and Figure

# Acknowledgments

Anyone writing a book about American government might well begin by acknowledging a debt to the Founding Fathers, who authored a novel constitution of republican government that has proven as durable as it is extraordinary. In addition, I would add thanks to those who lobbied successfully to establish the nation's capital on the banks of the Potomac, thus creating a company town with an industry that should interest every professor of politics. Since undergraduate days at Johns Hopkins in Baltimore twenty-five years ago, I have always enjoyed visits to Washington, walking the streets and parks, admiring its town planning and vernacular architecture, and utilitarian aspects of the buildings that house federal cafeterias.

One of the many attractive things about Washington is the people who live there. As the dedication makes clear, the author became indebted to them in the four years of preliminary research leading up to this study, and in the twelve months of intensive work that followed, for their readiness to share their political insights at all hours, from 7:30 in the morning until rather later than that at night. Any social scientist expects and normally finds keen intelligence and fluency with ideas in a university setting. It is doubly satisfying to meet men who combine with this a considerable firsthand experience of practical problems of governing, and use language as expressive and as American as anything found in Mark Twain or Ring Lardner. In the quotations that punctuate this book, I have tried to give a feeling for the ways in which public officials, speaking off the record, offer vivid and clear insights into human nature and politics.

In the course of some seventy-two interviews with present and former White House staff, officials at all levels of the Office of Management and Budget, and officials in a variety of positions in fourteen federal agencies, I was fortunate enough to acquire many unpublished materials relating to the main themes of this study. It is important to set what is said on paper in dry and sometimes tortured form against what is said face to face, in order to draw together both formal and informal aspects of the process of governing. Each form of documentation has its own reality: ideas can be made extremely interesting in conversation, yet rapidly lose their force when written down in an HEW program manual. Similarly, statements contained in an interoffice memorandum may seem just so much filler, until someone points out the political significance lying behind carefully worded, albeit seemingly opaque clauses. This study draws extensively upon unpublished OMB and departmental documentation arising from the first two years of the program for monitoring Presidential objectives; it also makes use of unpublished studies of the organization of the Bureau of the Budget/OMB, and of the Heineman Commission's Report on Government Organization of 1967. In addition, federal librarians of the Office of Management and Budget and at the United States Civil Service Commission, who truly deserve their name of information specialists, were of substantial assistance in tracking down documents and information buried in the morass of materials pouring forth from the Government Printing Office.

In acknowledging individuals whose insights and comments have proven useful, it is best to leave anonymous the great bulk of present and former federal officials who have provided assistance and comment in many ways. Those political scientists and in-and-outers who can be given public recognition are acknowledged here by name. In particular, I am grateful to the following for valuable comments made, and repeated, until the full force of their points registered: William H. Brill, Thomas E. Cronin, Erwin Hargrove, Edwin Harper, Joel Havemann, Hugh Heclo, Stephen Hess, Herbert Kaufman, John D. Lees, Brian Rapp, Allen Schick, Harold Seidman and, last and not least, Aaron Wildavsky.

The Woodrow Wilson International Center for Scholars, located in air-conditioned Romanesque splendor above the Mall, provided an appropriately congenial and neutral base from which to commence research in a Washington where too many trails led to the modern horror of the Watergate. I am grateful to the entire staff of the Center, from the Director, Dr. James H. Billington, to the guards who cheered me on my way as I signed out late at night and on weekends, for the hospitality and support provided. I am also grateful to the John Simon Guggenheim Foundation for providing the Fellowship which guaranteed time off from routine University responsibilities of teaching politics, so I could learn something about its practice in Washington, and to the University of Strathclyde for leave of absence. Once again, Mrs. R. West of the Department of Politics at the University of Strathclyde demonstrated her superb skills. As one bystander commented, "Why, she can type faster than the Professor can write." Mrs. M. McGlone also made things move much easier, by looking after many things while my mind (and sometimes my body) was some three thousand miles away.

Not least, I appreciate the patience of my wife and children who not only had to put up with the fact that their father was writing another book, but that he was away in America to do it. May they come to appreciate the great Republic, and not least, its capital city, as their father has done.

Richard Rose

University of Strathclyde,
Glasgow

# Managing Presidential Objectives

# 1

# In Search of
# Political Objectives

*It is the goals of management that are important; the tools become
important only as they aid in reaching these goals. In recent years it has
become more and more difficult to determine the objective that management seeks to achieve.*

Harold Smith, Director, Bureau of the Budget, 1945

Does government have objectives? If so, *what* are they? *Whose* are
they? How can anyone—citizen, public official or even President—
know what these objectives are? The answer to the first question
seems obvious. Of course, governments have objectives. But the
answers to the questions that follow are neither obvious nor agreed;
they concern both power and purpose. Anyone who states political
objectives (that is, what government ought to be doing) enters the
field of political controversy; the actions he proposes, as well as his
claim to speak for government, will be disputed. To conclude that
government has no objectives is to imply equally arguable propositions: government is directionless, the actions of politicians are
devoid of any public purpose, and the impact of government upon
society is the by-product of events, rather than the result of conscious intent.

   If government has objectives, how do we know what they are?
The objectives of the United States federal government are nowhere
set down in print, as is done with the budget of the United States or
the laws that constitute the United States Code. From time to time,
Presidents or Presidential aspirants call for or produce a statement of
national objectives. But none of these statements of national goals

1

has ever had any significant political impact. The preamble to the Constitution has survived so long as a statement of national objectives because of the vagueness of its statements, e.g.: "promote the general welfare." Political commentators may impute objectives to government, whether the imputations are flattering, "helping people to help themselves," contentious, "redistribute income," or unflattering, "serve the interests of some conspiratorial group." Whatever one thinks of the persuasiveness of such statements, they remain but matters of conjecture.

Identifying political objectives seems simple enough at first sight. But in the search for political objectives one confronts or stumbles over political issues of fundamental importance, going far beyond the simplifications that form the rhetoric of political promises or, for that matter, of social scientists promising techniques to help politicians manage their work better. Some of the questions raised by this inquiry cannot be finally settled, because they reflect disputes as old as the institutions of American government itself.

The rhetoric and obfuscation of politicians, the circumlocutions and recondite phraseology of legislation, and the gobbledygook of bureaucrats must be penetrated to see what if any meaning lies behind the frequent invocation of political objectives. Unfortunately, the term is usually employed without any clear meaning assigned to it. In this study, political *objectives* are the expression of political values in terms that may be realized in the immediately foreseeable future by or through government. The daily concerns of politicians about what they must do each day gain meaning insofar as they are related to objectives realizable before the end of a President's term of office. An objective may be meant to be achieved within a legislative session (to secure Congressional enactment of an anticrime bill); within the forthcoming fiscal year (to reduce the rise in the cost of living); or at the time of the next Presidential election (to win it).

The immediate objectives of politicians may or may not be linked to longer-term *goals* expressing political values that government may realize in the determinate but more distant future. A goal may be stated in relatively precise terms: the enactment and implementation of a particular "anticrime" bill endorsed by a given interest group. Or it may be stated in more general, but still clear terms: increasing the proportion of American energy consumption supplied by domestic energy sources. The length of time required to achieve a goal is less important than statement in a form clear enough to show how one might get there from here. The steps needed to achieve a clearly stated goal can then be divided into a series of more immediate political objectives.

Politicians often prefer to discuss ideals, rather than anything so mundane as immediate objectives or clear goals. Political *ideals* are principles or conditions that cannot be completely realized—in this world, at least—with the knowledge and resources that governments today have in hand: "the abolition of crime in American society," or "a fair and adequate standard of living for all citizens of planet earth." Ideals are invoked without any intention of achievement through a burst of energy in 100 days, or the methodicalness of a five-year plan. While ideals are literally Utopian, they may nonetheless influence immediate choices of objectives, insofar as they offer politicians cues to guide public policy at the moment.

A statement of political objectives is neither proof nor sure promise of achievement. As if the difficulties of getting things done within American government were not enough, politicians must also recognize that the condition of the American people cannot be determined solely by what government does. This fact is sometimes a cause for disappointment, as in the liberal reaction to the inadequacies of Great Society programs to achieve President Johnson's ideals. Yet it can also be a cause for satisfaction, as in the liberal reaction to the failure of President Nixon's White House to achieve all of its objectives and goals.

Politicians may state objectives and goals in an active or a reactive manner. In a Presidential campaign, a politician is likely to be active in the assertion of what he wants government to do. The evidence of the federal budget and the statute books indicates that most politicians carry this activist outlook into office, whatever their party label or nominal ideology. The demands made upon government are always numerous and loud enough to justify action, and activity is proof of the importance of a public person. Even a President committed to doing as little as he might, such as Dwight D. Eisenhower, had to react to issues put before him for decision. When a President defines objectives in reaction to events, his values are not necessarily stated explicitly; they are the preferences implicit in the pattern of choices that he makes. While a biographer may concentrate attention upon the motives leading an individual to act, a student of government will look first at the objectives and at their consequences. It is these, rather than individual motives, that directly affect the world about us.

Many social scientists take for granted that the objectives of politicians and of government are clearly and easily identified; they then proceed to erect elaborate theories describing how governments can or should achieve them. (Cf. Rose, 1973) The most ambitious social scientists impute functions to government, that is, goals that it should continuously strive toward. The directing force may not be the conscious choice of individuals, but rather, a "hidden hand" that guides social processes, in addition to or in spite of government. For example, government may be said to perform the function of societal goal-attainment, complementing other institutions in society concerned with adaptation, pattern maintenance, and social integration. Government may be assumed to be primarily concerned with mobilizing a nation's aggregate resources—or with reconciling conflicting interests between groups within society. Even such political functions as rule making, rule application and rule adjudication may be attributed to government. Such statements may or may not be useful to social scientists in developing a functionalist theory of government. They are of virtually no use in conducting the everyday affairs of government, for they leave indeterminate the chief questions facing governors: what are their specific objectives and goals, and how can they be reached?

One group of political scientists, starting from the simple assumption that the goal of a political party is to maximize its chance of winning an election, has prescribed perpetual campaign strategies far more refined and mathematically complex than any real-life politician is likely to comprehend, let alone follow as a "how to do it guide" to success in his work.

Economists have assumed that the chief problem for governors is to determine the relative costs and benefits of different objectives, or different means to an agreed goal. Cost-benefit analysis was introduced into the federal government in the belief that such an economic calculus would help public officials provide the most benefits for the fewest bucks. The experience of economists in government has made evident many problems in the measurement of the benefits and costs of public policies, and in the identification of political objectives.

The systems analysts who spread from the Department of Defense throughout federal agencies in the mid-1960s with the introduction of Planning Program Budgeting System (PPBS) made the identification of objectives their first priority. In the words of a senior RAND Corporation official:

> The first and most important task of the analyst is to discover what the decision-maker's objectives are (or should be) and then how to measure the extent to which these objectives are, in fact, attained by various choices. This done, strategies, policies or possible actions can be examined, compared, and recommended on the basis of how well and how cheaply they can accomplish these objectives. (Quade, 1966: 249)

The quotation is characteristic of the confidence of economists in the prescriptive validity of their techniques, in that the author leaves open whether the analyst's role is to describe objectives that a politician has, or to tell him what they should be. One moral of the PPBS experiment is that politicians do not wish to have their objectives prescribed to them by men with doctorates in economics.

Sociologists have been encouraged to assume that government has objectives, by being commissioned to evaluate newly established welfare programs to see how well they are achieving their objectives. The first thing they learn is that there is no list of easily measured objectives at hand, whether published to the world in the language of Congressional intent, or secreted from public view by a bureaucrat prone to duplicity. The author of a standard textbook on evaluation research comments: "Program goals are often hazy, ambiguous, hard to pin down. Occasionally, the official goals are merely a long list of pious and partly incompatible platitudes." (Weiss, 1972: 25)

Political scientists with firsthand experience of government are almost invariably sceptical about the existence of political objectives. At least four reasons may be advanced to explain why governments do not and cannot have objectives in any meaningful sense of the word.

Any statement of political objectives is likely to be so *vague* that it cannot discern the conditions meant to be realized. In other words, objectives are often ambiguous symbols, suffusing an area of controversy with words that mean different things to different men. There is an immediate incentive to politicians to keep their objectives vague. In this way, many different groups can think that a politician favors what they want or, at the least, is not committed to oppose their wishes. Precise objectives can stimulate controversy and opposition. A politician who commits himself to a precise objective loses status if he fails, whereas a politician whose objectives are vague can never be proven to have failed in his aspirations. Obfuscating objectives is not confined to the politically weak. Consider the following comment from a senior official in the Executive Office of the President: "Presidential statements should be soft, fluid, vague, even tricky. There should be nothing in them to attract flak. We spend hours constructing paragraphs so that afterwards we can interpret them different ways to different clients."*

Political objectives are *multiple*, because in aggregate the concerns of government are multitudinous and the responsibilities of individual officeholders large as well. An individual politician is better off spreading his concerns among a multiplicity of objectives. In this way he has a chance of making progress in some areas, even while stymied in others. By seeking to do many things, he can claim that he is doing something for every one of his constituents. Congressmen typically hedge their bets, enunciating broad, vague objectives, while simultaneously helping constituents who write their office gain personal benefits from government.

*Quotations appearing without attribution came from seventy-two interviews that the author conducted with senior career officials and Presidential appointees in the federal executive in Washington in 1974-1975.

By shifting emphasis from one objective to another quickly and unexpectedly, a politician creates *instability*. Mobility is the salvation of a politician hard pressed to do things. He can try to exert influence where it is most likely to have some effect at the moment. By waiting until support for a program has crystallized, he can be sure of declaring objectives that will enhance rather than detract from his popularity. Even better, by delaying support for a program until after it has been enacted and proven popular, a politician can be a "risk-free" proponent of government activities. In any event, the pressure of office insures that few politicians are able to concentrate exclusively upon a single objective for a term of office. They must go where the action is, and the multitudinous demands of government will keep them moving. The pressures are worst upon the Presidency. One White House official, after a month on the job, commented, "I didn't realize that this was a place where everything hit the fan before 9 o'clock *every* morning."

The pursuit of a variety of objectives, some vague and some precise, makes the sum total of a politician or a governor's actions appear *confusing or contradictory*. They will appear confusing if there is no consistent theme or themes running through a multiplicity of objectives, e.g., "providing benefits for the poor" and "maintaining the world's strongest armed services." A government's objectives will appear contradictory if some actions are intended to redistribute income to the poor, while others benefit the wealthy. The Congressional practice of "log rolling" makes sense to individual Congressmen, for one can vote for another's objective, without interest in its substantive impact, in return for the latter's vote for his particular concern. But the sum total of a series of government actions taken by log rolling gets the lumberjacks nowhere—except insofar as the logs they stand on are carried forward by the force of the river's current.

To try to identify the objectives of government—an institution that aggregates actions of hundreds of politicians—is to compound the foregoing tendencies. To describe the objectives of government as vague, multiple, unstable, and confusing and contradictory is not to argue that government has no objectives, but rather that it has *too many* objectives to be comprehended or integrated by a single mind or a single institution within government. This is but another way of making the point that the concept of "government" is itself vague, multiple, unstable, confusing, and contradictory. The word can point to many different institutions, each of which constitutes a part of government. As the point of reference changes, so too should we change our expectations of its objectives. To state that there is no single objective pervasively guiding government activities at a given moment, or that there is no single set of relatively clear and coordinated objectives directing government in a given four-year period is but to say that there is no single central individual or institution giving direction to American government.

Because this is a book about problems of management, it is a study of objectives in an organizational setting rather than a study of individual concerns. One cannot deduce organizational objectives solely from interviewing a cross section of individuals who work for an organization, or even by studying the President of an organization, whether the federal government or something slightly simpler. The federal government is a complex institution. To understand what its activities are about, one must combine an awareness of individual objectives and institutional forms. It is by virtue of office in an institution that the objectives of the President become more significant than the wishes of any one of 200 million other Americans. What is true of the President is true, to a lesser extent, of Presidential appointees throughout the federal executive, and also of high-ranking career officials. Collectively, these are the people, insofar as any individual can, who determine the direction of collective action. To give direction to government, individuals must learn the art of joining their personal objectives with those of institutions, whether a political party, a Congressional committee, a government agency or the White House itself. An individual's objectives are more often influenced by the established commitments and priorities of the organization to which he belongs than are its goals determined by his individual preferences.

American government is conventionally depicted as an organization identifying and realizing popular objectives and goals in theories of political representation. Individual voters choose between two parties offering candidates for the Presidency and Congress. The platform adopted by each party at its Presidential nominating convention sets out party objectives, goals, and ideals. Notwithstanding many reasons that can be offered for parties avoiding clear commitments in platform statements, there is nonetheless evidence that party politicians do in fact achieve many of their platform objectives. (See Pomper, 1968; David, 1971) Congressmen give statutory authority to popular objectives by legislation. Insofar as the objectives of legislation are vague, multiple, confusing and contradictory, Congress transfers to the executive branch the power to determine what specifically the legislation will try to accomplish, subject to the influence of continuing oversight by Congressional committees.

While elected officeholders have the legitimate authority and formal power to identify objectives through legislation, appropriations, the appointment process, and other prerogatives, they do not have the power to realize the objectives themselves. This task is normally in the hands of career officials, whether in the executive branch or operating federally authorized and funded programs in state and local government. Elected officeholders achieve their objectives by influencing bureaucrats with "hands on" control of government operations.

The specification of objectives is one among several important techniques that the legitimate governors of society can use in their effort to give direction to government. If a President keeps his objectives and goals secret, then career officials cannot know what the President expects of them unless they are in face-to-face contact with the White House. In order to extend influence beyond those individuals whom he sees personally, a President must give some indication of what he wishes done in a form that can be transmitted to officials distant from the White House, and thus, subject to public disclosure, whether authorized or otherwise. The less clear, the less practical, and the more contradictory and confusing a set of objectives are, then the greater the uncertainty about the meaning of a Presidential directive. From the President's point of view, this means that lower-echelon officials can not act in ways determined by his objectives. From a career official's perspective, insofar as objectives are uncertain, the power of discretionary choice has been transferred to his hands.

The objectives of transient elected officials—and the President is far more transient than a senior Congressman—are not the only things that concern career officials. A literal translation of the term "bureaucracy" would suggest that it is their objectives, rather than those of formal political leaders, that rule. Bureaucratic objectives concerning the career interests of civil servants and the status of their bureau need not necessarily be in conflict with broader political objectives. For example, a President dependent upon the vote of farm states is likely to have objectives consistent with the wish of officials in the Department of Agriculture to expand their organization and their programs. Studies of foreign affairs illustrate, however, that organizational processes and bureaucratic politics lead different groups close to the President to promote competing objectives for the nation's common defense. (See e.g., Allison, 1971; Halperin, 1974)

At lower levels of government, officials do not see their work so much in terms of actively seeking objectives (whether political or bureaucratic) but rather in terms of passively carrying out prescribed duties or organizational functions. (Rose, 1974: 120f) For example, an elevator operator in a federal building is not trying to "carry the government to great heights"; his duty is to respond to a bell when it is rung. At intermediate levels, career officials may exercise discretion within circumscribed areas, for example, when processing requests for grants authorized by an Act of Congress that specifies some but not all criteria for eligibility. In addition to legislation, duties can be set by professional training (e.g., of engineers or public health officials) or by on-the-job training, formally and informally socializing an individual into the norms of his organization. However established, such duties are important insofar as they introduce a degree of predictability into actions for which elected officeholders are formally responsible. These routine duties are not related to the dynamic objectives of politicians, but rather to highly specialized and relatively persisting institutions of government.

At the highest level of the bureaucracy, in so-called supergrade or executive level posts, career officials find themselves working closely with Presidential appointees on matters involving substantial discretion in deciding what to do, as well as how to realize objectives. In such posts, individuals do not "go political" by accepting appointments that require them to abandon their career status; instead, they go political by adopting the outlook and sensitivities of men themselves defining political objectives. In the open, easily permeated structure of the executive branch, high-ranking officials are made to feel political pressures from Congress and interest groups, as well as from Presidential appointees above them.

In such circumstances, the problem of managing the executive branch is seen, not as a problem of technique, but rather in its real political terms: identifying the objectives that government should seek to achieve. The American system of government has no central authoritative figure—a Cabinet, a King or a dictator—to enunciate, safe from effective challenge, what the chief political objectives of government are at any time. The political process involves competition and conflict between individuals and groups, each with some objectives. The joint product of their efforts is more likely to blur than to clarify the meaning of what government does. Moreover, the forces causing confusion in government at the end of World War II—an increasingly complicated environment changing at an increasing speed and increasingly buffeted by influences from every corner of the world—have become far stronger since Harold Smith (1945: 29) diagnosed them in Washington thirty years ago.

One of the persisting features of the Presidency of Richard M. Nixon was that the White House sought, in various and sometimes dubious ways, to come to grips with the problem of giving direction to government. The Nixon Presidency was distinctive in that the means chosen to this political end were administrative, rather than legislative or based upon appeals through the mass media. (See Nathan, 1975) This effort to innovate reveals much about the persisting characteristics of political institutions, for the success or failure of any innovation depends not only upon its intrinsic qualities, but also upon established patterns of behavior in the institution which is meant to be reformed.

Early in 1973 President Nixon, then at the momentary height of his powers, took the final step in his five-year campaign to change the organization as well as the programs of the federal executive; the President announced the introduction of management by objectives throughout the executive branch. This initiative made the broad philosophical questions discussed in this chapter of immediate concern to high-ranking public officials in Washington. The White House not only assumed that the government had objectives, but also, that they could be identified. It asked department heads to identify its chief Presidential objectives so that the Office of Management and Budget (OMB) could then monitor agency performance to see whether the results of their actions were consistent with the objectives endorsed. For an agency head to tell the President that his department could not identify any objectives would be tantamount to confessing that he did not know what he was trying to do. The object of this book is to examine, carefully and intensively, what the introduction of this new management technique into government can teach us about the persisting problem of political objectives.

To argue that it is meaningless to ascribe objectives to government is to imply that government is uncontrollable, that is, that politicians and career public officials do not know what they want to do, how to do what they are supposed to be doing, or why they should try to get things done. The denizens of public offices, including the White House, do not individually display apathy or indecisiveness as they go about their individual pursuits, even though the collective product of individual efforts may be something else again. In the aftermath of Watergate, Americans may take some solace from evidence that the pathologies of government make it difficult for it to do everything that high-placed public officials sometimes want to do. But these difficulties also inhibit government when it undertakes things that citizens can only achieve by collective action, from defending the country against foreign aggressors or the disturbances of the international economic system through conserving or controlling the environment to providing social security benefits financed by taxes levied for welfare purposes.

All that we know for sure is that government has activities. Millions of civil servants, billions of dollars of public funds, tens of thousands of pages of laws and regulations and the myriad organizations charged with enforcing them do not remain inert. The daily routines of public officials constitute the basic stuff (some would say, trivia) of government. These actions are not undertaken in a political vacuum. They constitute the goods and ills that government provides in response to popular demands. Activities on the scale of the American government in the 1970s cannot occur without some impact upon society at large, the ultimate consumer of government's outputs. Even if actions of government are without identifiable or intended objectives, they are not without consequences.

# 2

# Giving Direction
# to Government

*A President need not be a man of brilliant intellectual gifts. Eloquence, imagination, profundity of thought or extent of knowledge are not necessary for the due discharge in ordinary times of the duties of his post. Four-fifths of his work is the same kind as that which devolves on the chairman of a commercial company or the manager of a railway.*

James Bryce, 1888

*If you were Secretary of Transportation, the business of making the trains run on time wouldn't be so simple as it looks.*

Office of Management and Budget official

The problem facing a political leader is the same in any government, whether the pluralistic structure of the United States or the formal monolith of the Soviet Union: how to influence officials beneath him, so that *their* actions will contribute to the achievement of *his* objectives. In any large organization, whether the Ford Motor Company or a heterogeneous conglomerate, such as Litton Industries or the Department of Health, Education and Welfare, the man on top trades hands on direction of one operating program for broader responsibilities. The higher a man's formal position, the less time he can devote to any one responsibility, and the more important it is for him to achieve his objectives through influencing other people. The President of the United States is in an extreme position, because he is one man sitting on top of a federal executive with 2.7 million civilian employees. The problems of the President are matched to a considerable degree by those facing Cabinet officers and agency heads. To rule as well as reign within the executive branch of government, a political leader must cultivate techniques that give him *hausmacht*, an apt German term meaning "power in one's realm."

A newly elected President acquires, in his role as Chief Executive, responsibility for a vast hodgepodge of activities, each the particular ongoing concern of a government bureau and of a group in Congress. Some he will have supported in a previous political role, and others opposed. Many will be the work of political leaders who have long since passed from the Washington scene. The President must accept them all: they go with the job, just like Air Force 1, the use of Camp David, and the heat of the Washington summer.

Inertia directs the bulk of what government does. The concept of inertia is ambiguous. It can refer to something that is at rest, or to steady motion that will continue until acted upon by an external force. The inertia activities of government involve continuing motion. The daily activities of public officials involve the enforcement of thousands of laws, the disbursement of hundreds of millions of dollars, and tens of thousands of discretionary decisions taken in accord with routine responsibilities. Just as an economy that has a constant gross national product nonetheless engages in ceaseless activity to stay where it is, so the institutions of government, even when doing nothing new, are also centers of continuous and continuing activities. For example, the routine administration of millions of social security benefits is bureaucratic activity on a great scale. As long as the bureaucrats in charge avoid controversy, politicians need give its work little time or thought. But let social security clerks go on strike or computers fail to print out monthly checks and the administration of social security would suddenly become of first priority in Washington.

Inertia is a constraint upon a President. He may wish to secure action, whereas bureaucrats may wish to leave things as they are. If the President doubts the powerful forces maintaining routine activities of government, he need only try to introduce changes to see how strong are the forces carrying it on its established ways. Inertia can be positively harmful when a public agency is routinely moving in a direction that political leaders regard as disastrous. Yet a President can also view inertia as a potential asset. If only he can once succeed in getting Congress to enact a new law and appropriate funds to operate a new program, there is then every likelihood that the program will be driven by inertia long after his Administration has left the White House, and even after his party has lost control of the executive branch.

The variety and magnitude of the inertia activities of government can be roughly indicated by three different measures: public laws, public expenditure, and public officials. These indicators register the extent to which the government is committed by law to act, the money resources it has at hand and, equally important, the numbers of people whose everyday job is to do the work of government. A brief review of these commitments will not capture the full flavor and range of activities of the federal government. It will, however, indicate what flashes by the President when he first begins to contemplate the things that are going on in "his" Administration—whether he gives them any direction or not.

In his oath of office the President swears to uphold the laws of the United States, and to see that they are faithfully executed. No one in the White House ever reads straight through the dozens of volumes of the United States Code, the body of laws that the President has sworn to uphold. The President is much more concerned with the legislation described in his State of the Union message. But a State of the Union message is brief by comparison with the United States Code. It is also hypothetical, a statement of the laws that the President would like to see passed, rather than a record of what is already there to be carried out.

The most succinct overview of the laws of the United States is given in the table of contents of the United States Code. To list the 49 titles and 1507 chapters by which laws are classified requires twenty-six pages. The chapters of the U.S. Code give some flavor of the commitments that the President inherits. The catalog in Table 2.1 is a much condensed version of the full table of contents; it lists by name the title headings of the Code and tabulates the 1507 chapter headings into which the contents are divided. Sixty per cent of the activities with which every Administration must concern itself by law are among necessary responsibilities of any modern government—foreign policy and defense, law enforcement, finance and taxation, and the organization and procedure of government (Categories A, C, D, G). Such laws range from questions of war and national defense and customs to measures concerning such symbols as the American flag and seal, and public printing and documents. The range of laws concerning the regulation of commerce, industry, and natural resources makes an Administration act not only against the natural environment, where agencies such as the National Aeronautical and Space Administration have been notably successful, but also, against industries, labor unions, and national and international economic forces, where the influences of the federal government is uncertain. Laws concerning social welfare are relatively few in quantity, and jumble together social security legislation with provision for a motley collection of federal homes, national cemeteries, and wards of government in such places as St. Elizabeth's Hospital and the Columbia Institution for the Deaf.

If public expenditure is thought to be the best indicator of the continuing activities of government, then the federal budget provides the wealth of data indicating the ongoing commitments of government. Particularly noteworthy here is that each year's budget contains an estimate of the proportion of the budget that is uncontrollable, representing payments due individuals under existing laws, such as social security benefits and interest on the national debt, as well as costs fixed in prior years by contractual obligations. In fiscal year 1974 relatively uncontrollable items in budget outlays accounted for 72 percent of federal expenditure. Moreover, the proportion of relatively uncontrollable expenditure has been growing in the past decade; in 1967, it amounted to 59 per cent of total federal spending. (Budget, 1975: 355) A President has a little more leeway than these figures indicate, for he, like his predecessors, can request that Congress appropriate money to be spent after the forthcoming budget year. In his request for the 1976 budget, President Ford asked for authority to spend $385 billion; of this, 38 per cent was earmarked for spending in future years. He had reason to feel justified in passing on commitments to the future, for his predecessors had left him with future obligations to spend $493 billion, sums authorized before President Ford had yet to submit his first budget. (Budget, 1975: 23)

Public expenditure figures are presented to the President in two ways—subdivided by government department (e.g., Defense, Interior, HUD, etc.) or by nominal function (i.e., national defense, natural resources, environment and energy, etc.). The primary emphasis in the budget review process is upon spending by departments and agencies within government, and not upon expenditure by function. The Office of Management and Budget is organized to review proposals from departments and not to review functions in the abstract. The functional categories of the budget are derived post hoc, as a supplementary classification of expenditure requests originating from departments and allocated to departments. In other words, a President can be sure *who* spends the money, but he cannot be sure what function or consequences such expenditure has.

Analyzing public expenditure by agency emphasizes the importance of the social welfare concerns of government. The biggest spending department of the federal government in 1974 was Health, Education and Welfare, accounting for 30.5 per cent of the federal budget, substantially more than is spent on defense. Big expenditure is not, however, necessary to make a subject important. The State Department has the smallest budget of any Cabinet department, and yet is not least in significance. Nor does the large expenditure of the Veterans Administration upon relatively uncontrollable benefits confer high political status upon that agency.

What is most relevant here is the extent to which budget expenditure is relatively unchangeable from year to year. President Ford inherited commitments from President Nixon that resulted in $330.04 billion being spent in the fiscal year ending on June 30,

**TABLE 2.1.** Government Activities: *the Commitment in Law*

| TITLE HEADING OF THE U.S. CODE | CHAPTER HEADINGS $N^a$ | Total % |
|---|---|---|
| A) Foreign Policy and Defense | | |
| Arbitration | 2 | |
| Armed Forces (including Navy) | 195 | |
| Coast Guard | 12 | |
| Foreign Relations | 47 | |
| Uniformed Services Pay | 11 | |
| Veterans Benefits | 31 | |
| War and National Defense | 116 | |
| (7) | 414 | 27.5 |
| B) Regulation of Commerce and Industry | | |
| Agriculture | 68 | |
| Bankruptcy | 15 | |
| Commerce and Trade | 62 | |
| Copyright | 3 | |
| Food and Drug | 16 | |
| Highways | 5 | |
| Intoxicating Liquor | 10 | |
| Labor | 19 | |
| Patents | 17 | |
| Postal Service | 18 | |
| Railroads | 15 | |

| TITLE HEADING OF THE U.S. CODE | CHAPTER HEADINGS $N$ | Total % |
|---|---|---|
| D) Law and Order | | |
| Crime and Criminal Procedure | 104 | |
| Judiciary and Judicial Procedure | 59 | |
| National Guard | 4 | |
| (3) | 167 | 11.1 |
| E) Natural Resources | | |
| Conservation | 56 | |
| Mineral Lands and Mining | 25 | |
| Navigation and Navigable Waters | 28 | |
| Public Lands | 39 | |
| (4) | 148 | 9.8 |
| F) Social Concerns | | |
| Education | 41 | |
| Hospitals, Asylums and Cemeteries | 10 | |
| Public Health and Welfare | 79 | |
| (3) | 130 | 8.6 |

| | N | % |
|---|---|---|
| Shipping | 38 | |
| Telegraphs, Telephones and Radiotelephones | 7 | |
| Transportation | 26 | |
| (14) | 319 | 21.2 |

| G) Finance and Taxation | | |
|---|---|---|
| Banks and Banking | 25 | |
| Customs | 12 | |
| Internal Revenue Code | 52 | |
| Money and Finance | 25 | |
| (4) | 114 | 7.6 |

| Totals | 1507 | 100.1[b] |
|---|---|---|

| C) Organization and Procedure of Government | | |
|---|---|---|
| General Provisions | 3 | |
| Congress | 17 | |
| The President | 4 | |
| Flag and Seal, Seat of Govt. | 5 | |
| Government Organization and Employees | 33 | |
| Surety | 1 | |
| Aliens and Nationality | 13 | |
| Census | 5 | |
| Indians | 17 | |
| Patriotic Societies and Observances | 55 | |
| Public Buildings, Property and Works | 20 | |
| Public Contracts | 6 | |
| Printing and Documents | 19 | |
| Territories and Insular Possessions | 17 | |
| (14) | 215 | 14.3 |

Source: *United States Code* (1973: Supplement 2, p. v. *et seg.*)
[a] In this and subsequent tables, N refers to the number of cases tabulated.
[b] Percentages do not always add up to 100.0% because of rounding off.

1974. The budget for fiscal year 1975 had been before Congress for six months, and in part had already been acted upon. Moreover, the 'process of drafting the budget for fiscal year 1976 had already commenced. The President had five months—and many other demands upon his time—in which to draft the first budget presented in the name of his Administration. What is of most significance in the resulting document is not the increase in cash expenditure, for this is to be expected in a period of cost inflation. Instead, it is the changes in departmental appropriations as a share in the total budget. These had altered by 13.6 per cent in the two-year period, illustrating the extent to which inertia forces give direction to public expenditure. The President can only make incremental changes. (See also Davis, Dempster and Wildavsky, 1966)

TABLE 2.2.  Government Activities: *the Commitment of Money*

| DEPARTMENT | 1974 ACTUAL AUTHORITY ($000,000) | FEDERAL BUDGET (TOTAL %) |
|---|---|---|
| Legislative Branch | 657 | 0.2 |
| The Judiciary | 213 | 0.1 |
| Executive Office of the President | 97 | 0.03 |
| Funds appropirated to the President | 12,430 | 3.8 |
| Agriculture | 13,144 | 4.0 |
| Commerce | 1,501 | 0.5 |
| Defense—military | 81,073 | 24.5 |
| Defense—civil | 1,779 | 0.5 |
| Health, Education and Welfare | 100,857 | 30.5 |
| Housing and Urban Development | 8,110 | 2.4 |
| Interior | 1,961 | 0.6 |
| Justice | 1,921 | 0.6 |
| Labor | 10,640 | 3.2 |
| State | 841 | 0.2 |
| Transportation | 17,627 | 5.3 |
| Treasury | 36,033 | 10.9 |
| Energy Research and Development Administration | 2,475 | 0.7 |
| Environmental Protection Agency | 5,952 | 1.8 |
| General Services Administration | −471[a] | (0.1) |
| NASA | 3,037 | 0.9 |
| Veterans Administration | 13,939 | 4.2 |
| Other independent agencies | 16,724 | 5.0 |
| Totals | $330,040,000,000 | 100.03 |

(Figures are gross, omitting deductions for offsetting receipts totalling $16,650 million in 1974, and an estimated $20,193 million in 1976)

*Source:* Budget, 1975: 323.
[a] Revenue exceeds expenditure.

The number of civil service personnel is a third indicator of the ongoing activities to which any President is committed. Unlike the President, civil servants have a permanent claim on their office. The federal government is today the largest single employer of manpower in the United States. It has 2.7 million civilian employees, and an additional 2.5 million military personnel. It is also committed to underwrite the employment of millions more, whether working in such para-state institutions as AMTRAK, as private sector employees of companies almost exclusively concerned with supplying goods to the federal government, or as state and local government officials whose salaries are met from federal funds.

The scale of departmental activity is indicated by the respective numbers of employees. Table 2.3 calls attention to the enormous disparities in manpower employed in different government departments. The massive numbers of employees in Defense and HEW are consistent with their eminence in spending and political significance,

**TABLE 2.3.** Government Activities: *the Commitment of Personnel*

| | PERSONNEL | |
| AGENCY | Senior | Total |
|---|---|---|
| Defense | 1,614 | 1,074,120 |
| State | 1,077 | 33,566 |
| Health, Education and Welfare | 721 | 144,110 |
| NASA | 639 | 27,069 |
| Commerce | 542 | 35,930 |
| Justice | 489 | 51,247 |
| Transportation | 420 | 74,025 |
| Treasury | 417 | 118,195 |
| Atomic Energy Commission | 365 | 8,140 |
| Veterans Administration | 314 | 208,673 |
| Agriculture | 305 | 124,155 |
| Interior | 288 | 81,437 |
| Labor | 175 | 14,146 |
| Environmental Protection Agency | 148 | 10,999 |
| Housing and Urban Development | 145 | 17,239 |
| National Science Foundation | 145 | 1,373 |
| General Services Administration | 101 | 40,226 |
| Civil Service Commission | 62 | 7,977 |
| Postal Service | 53 | 706,688 |
| Small Business Administration | 42 | 4,731 |
| ACTION | 42 | 2,008 |
| Totals | 8,104 | 2,786,054 |

*Source:* U.S. Civil Service Commission Bureau of Executive Manpower, unpublished statistics for June, 1974.

just as the low numbers in the Small Business Administration and ACTION reflect the lesser political importance of their work. Yet there are inconsistencies: the Postal Service is the second largest government employer, and the Treasury ranks well below the Veterans Administration in size. One way to discriminate between agencies that are large because of routine work and those that perform "big" tasks is to rank them according to the number of senior staff employed, that is, supergrade civil servants (GS 16 to 18 ratings), executive level staff, and others in equivalent grades. Insofar as organizations with lots of high-ranking personnel have a claim to be regarded as themselves important, Defense, State, and HEW occupy the leading positions, and the mammoth Postal Service is third from the bottom. The State Department, though small in total personnel, has almost as many senior staff as the ten lowest federal agencies combined, ranging from ACTION to Interior. (Table 2.3)

Laws, money, and manpower collectively reflect the ongoing activities of the federal government. Acts of one Congress remain in force unless repealed. Departments give organizational form to past commitments. Civil servants have lifetime appointments, rather than serving on annually renewable contracts or at a month's notice of dismissal. Headings in the budget are virtually uncontrollable commitments by government to continue spending money on established programs, varying the amounts by limited increments from year to year. Not least in importance, the benefits provided by government create expectations among their recipients that they will continue. These popular expectations are a strong force maintaining government activities from year to year.

As long as inertia forces are pushing government in the direction a President wishes it to go, this provides him with the most economical way possible to manage the great bulk of the activities of government. The "automatic pilot" of institutionalized inertia gives clear and predictable direction. If the President does not like the direction in which inertia tends to push his Administration, then he can seek to alter it or, alternatively, resign himself to the stoic acceptance of inertia tendencies as his own objectives. Only by ignoring *almost* everything that government does can the President find time and resources in which to identify and pursue a finite number of political objectives of his own.

Political leadership is leadership by exception. A President lets many things be run by the force of inertia, in order to be able to disturb routines where he believes inertia is dangerously misdirected and, even more importantly, to deal with all the non-routine problems forced upon his desk by events. The non-routine side of government will easily generate more than enough activity to keep the President occupied for the four-year life of an Administration. By definition, the course of government is uncertain or in dispute in non-routine situations. When events and policies are in flux, a President does not have to push against inertia. His problem is, instead, to direct government policy in the direction that he thinks best or, if this is not practicable, to make going with the trend of history his objective.

In giving direction to government, politicians emphasize questions of choice—what ought government to do?—rather than problems of management—how (or how well) do public officials carry out the work of government? The politician's conception of his role is aptly summed up in the motto: *to govern is to choose.*

The President is uniquely qualified to choose objectives for government. This is true whether he owes his office to endorsement by 43 or 61 per cent of the voters, or to the accidents of Vice Presidential appointment and succession. The President (and sometimes his Vice President) is the sole elected official within the executive branch of the federal government. Others who hold leadership positions there do so by virtue of Presidential appointment. The President can thus speak with an authority on behalf of the executive branch that is denied the hydra-headed Congress, which articulates its collective views by compositing the objectives of many different Representatives and Senators. The populace and the media look to the President for leadership in identifying what the whole of government ought to do to meet national problems. Increasingly, Congressmen and officials in state and local government also look to the White House to identify objectives for government action.

The choices of a President may initially be expressed in terms of ideals or distant and vague goals. If they are to have anything more than symbolic or rhetorical significance, they must be made "manageable," i.e., translated into more concrete statements of objectives to be realized and programs, i.e., specific government measures more or less clearly related to the objectives identified. The exigencies of politics often force politicians to act first and reflect afterwards. Immediate decisions become the stuff from which long-term consequences emerge—with or without any conscious choice of long-term objectives. A harassed President may even endorse a program, leaving others (himself included) to puzzle subsequently what his objective was in acting thus.

The President and Presidential appointees in the departments are directors of very large bureaucratic organizations, with complex institutions, long and easily attenuated lines of communications, and career officials who have their own objectives and far more years ahead of them in government than the Administration of the moment. In such circumstances, a President must delegate great authority to subordinates. In order to delegate while retaining influence upon what is done, a politician must indicate objectives and preferences that direct others' choices along *his* lines. To delegate authority without identifying objectives is to give subordinates the power to take decisions on their own account. In a bureaucratic setting, a President who avoids enunciating objectives is renouncing his potential to influence government. To choose objectives while disregarding what is done in consequence is also an empty kind of eminence.

Americans who look to the President to voice objectives that best reflect current political aspirations are interested in results, as well as in symbolic reassurance. If politics is promises, then government is ceaseless activity. The continuing ability of a President to satisfy rather than frustrate his followers depends upon the translation of his goals and objectives into programs, and the successful implementation of these programs. A President can blame Congress if Congress withholds legislation that he has requested. When the President secures the laws he requests to realize his objectives, then he must look within his own branch of government if failure nonetheless follows. A modern President's reputation is increasingly judged by whether his Administration can manage to deliver the results they promise, as well as by the good intentions and objectives that a President sets forth. In the words of an internal Bureau of the Budget (1967) report: "Future Presidents will also be administrative activists. They will be forced by the nature of the problems to try to run the government as well as make policy decisions." For a President, the problem is less a question of efficiency, that is, whether programs produce value in proportion to cost, than it is one of effectiveness, that is, whether intentions produce anything at all!

Questions of political choice and management interpenetrate; they do not remain in discrete boxes, as in an organization chart. No Congressman wants to have his name on a bill that turns out to be an administrative disaster, nor does a President relish the thought of spending much time and political capital in seeking a bill from Congress, only to find subsequently that the program brings him far more troubles than praise. Indecision in the federal government about establishing a national health insurance service illustrates how politicians may hesitate to make a choice, until they are confident that the alternative they select will not be an unmanageable monstrosity. The rising cost of health care for American citizens is a spur to action—just as the rising cost of existing federally funded health programs is a reminder of what can happen to government if the consequences of good intentions are not thought through before government makes commitments.

A President almost invariably concentrates upon questions of choice rather than management, because the task of determining his commitments and building coalitions to support positions taken is both important and exhausting. Seeking support for a bill requested in a State of the Union message is costly in terms of White House time, the compromises that must be made to attract necessary Congressional support, and commitments made to those who support what the White House wants in return for its support for what they want. Even within the executive branch, the process of negotiating the specific language and character of a bill can be almost endless. In the words of one official in the Executive Office: "Nobody ever says no in this town. They only give you qualifications. They say why don't you reshape it a little. Or why don't you go see x and y and z. Or why don't you wait a little while; we can't handle this right now. They can go on saying these things for the rest of your life."

By concentrating upon the choice and adoption of objectives, a President does what he is usually best qualified to do. There is nothing in the selection of a chief executive that insures that a President will have experience in the management of government. (Of Presidents since 1945, only Dwight D. Eisenhower—as a University head as well as an Army officer—had worked as an executive in a large organization). Stephen Hess explains, "Candidates do not turn management questions into campaign issues. Management is the structure of governance, not the substance of politics; campaigns are about politics, not governance." Scholars of the Presidency have similarly tended to ignore problems of steering the federal executive. Hess concludes (1974: 12, 20) "The reason for the treatment may be that management is outside the competence of those of us who regularly assess the Presidency." Once in office, a President is much more concerned with choosing what to do than he is with how these decisions are implemented (that is, how choices are turned into routine government activities) or the conduct of program activities on a continuing basis. A veteran observer of the federal executive diagnoses the situation thus:

> The history of management improvement in the federal government is a story of inflated rhetoric, shifting emphasis from one fashionable managerial skill to another, and a relatively low level of professional achievement. No President has been able to identify any significant political capital that might be made out of efforts to improve management except for the conservative purpose of economizing or reducing costs. (Bernstein, 1970: 515f)

The President's neglect of management concerns does not mean that management is unimportant. As one OMB management associate remarked in an interview, "Management *must be* important in any organization with 2.5 million employees." It is important to citizens, the consumers of government services, as well as to government employees. To ignore management and concentrate exclusively upon questions of choice is to risk rule by rhetoric, in which denunciations of problems are confused with the identification of solutions, and the passage of laws with records of achievement. Political leaders may give primary emphasis to where we ought to go. But their promises will be empty and, eventually, self-defeating, if they ignore questions of what is done to make the ship of state get there from here.

Even in terms of the President's own bias toward choice, management is important. The answer to the question facing any President— How much choice can I afford?—is: Only as much as you can carry out. A President may state "impossible" objectives only if he is sure that Congress will not endorse the aspirations that he has articulated. In such circumstances, Congress can bear the blame for the frustrations of a President's good intentions. The President (or his successor) is at risk, once Congress endorses objectives that the President has identified as his own. In such circumstances, not only has a President proposed what government ought to do, but also, as the head of the executive branch, he becomes responsible for what is in fact done to realize the objective. To arouse popular hopes by promoting an objective, only to have these aspirations denied by subsequent actions of government, is to achieve short-term political success at the cost of a long-term political loss in popular confidence in the effectiveness of government.

The distinction between choice and management is analytic, rather than practical. The two are parts of one continuing political process. One man's definition of politics may be another man's definition of management. Michael Oakeshott (1951: 8), a prominent English conservative philosopher, defines politics in terms that could equally be used by management experts to define their field: "the activity of attending to the general arrangements of a set of people." This relatively static view is found also in the definition of management contained in the first edition of the *International Encyclopedia of the Social Sciences:* "the process by which the execution of a given purpose is put into operation and supervised." (Sheldon, 1933: 77) A modern *Webster's Dictionary* (1963) offers almost interchangeable definitions of management—"judicious use of means to accomplish an end"—and politics—"the art or science concerned with guiding or influencing government policy."

Newer and more "activist" definitions of the direction of large organizations are found in both the literature of management and in the literature of politics. In the second edition of the *International Encyclopedia of the Social Sciences,* Cyert (1967: 249) defines management as choice: "the central core of the management function is decision-making behavior." David Easton's (1965: 50) well known definition of politics as "the authoritative allocation of values" similarly emphasizes the importance of choice. The political scientist and the management scientist both ignore the importance of getting choices carried out, whether within government or within a large private corporation.

The ambiguity in meaning goes back to the very origins of the words politics and management. The same Greek root, *polis*, appears in three different English words: politics, policy and police. To confine the study of politics to competition for elective office, as some journalists and political scientists do, is wrongfully to circumscribe our sense of what government is about. Policy is a term often used to refer to the activities and intentions of government in the broadest sense. When the modern state began in Europe several centuries ago, the police were responsible for the main policy concern of government, maintaining domestic order. (Cf. Chapman, 1970: 11ff) Today, the term public policy embraces a great variety of activities of public officials, and a heterogeneous range of ideas concerning what government ought to do.

The term "management" is derived from the Latin *manus*, hand. To manage a horse is to give direction to a horse by having one's hands on its reins. The idea of having one's hands on the reins of governmental power involves a practical as well as a metaphorical transmutation of meaning, for government is a menagerie of organizations, with many reins and hands grasping for them. In government or any large organization, the President does not execute actions with his own hands. In bureaucratic terminology, he is the chief among staff officers who direct those with "hands on" responsibilities. Line officials are immediately concerned with the day-to-day operations of government programs, in what are aptly described as operating agencies. The President or the Secretary in a large department such as HEW is "nonoperative," but he is not meant to be inoperative. His role is to give direction to line managers, and not to undertake particular activities themselves. Management is concerned with the implementation of what has been decided, and the regular monitoring of activities to make sure that what is happening now has been previously agreed and is still appropriate. Management focuses upon concrete program activities rather than choice in the abstract. It is not so much concerned with what might be chosen or what ought to be chosen, but with what does get done by government.

The most relevant definition of management in the context of Washington politics is found in such dictionary statements as "to make an organization serve one's purpose" or "to make and keep submissive." Harry Truman was speaking as a manager of men, and thus, as a manager of government, when he described the President's role thus: "I sit here all day trying to persuade people to do the things they ought to have sense enough to do without my persuading them. That's all the powers of the President amount to."

The language of management can sound familiarly like the language of power. A famous political science definition of power—"A has power over B to the extent that he can get B to do something that B would not otherwise do" (Dahl, 1957: 202f)—is paralleled by a definition of management cited in the *Oxford English Dictionary* (1936: 1197): "to make (a weapon, instrument, etc.) serve one's purpose." The crucial distinction between the two definitions is that Dahl describes power in terms of *personal* relationships, whereas the Oxford definition is suited to *impersonal* relationships in complex organizations such as government. (Cf. Rose, 1970: 155ff) Within the federal government, a single individual, even the President, cannot do many things himself, nor can he personally superintend many individuals who carry out activities in the name of the government. A President is not trying to command individuals, like an infantry lieutenant in the field. He is, instead, trying to make an alliance of nations concentrate upon the purposes that he thinks important, as well as (or instead of) the purposes important to individual members. (Cf. Olson, 1965) In domestic politics,* where collective action through complex organizations is the rule rather than the exception, one must learn to think of the President or a Presidential appointee exercising influence upon organizations. Rarely does anyone in the federal government have the power to do anything by himself; he uses such influence as he has in the hopes that, in conjunction with the actions of others, this will lead to collective action consistent with his wishes. (Cf. Hyneman, 1950: 39)

The pursuit of "power" or "influence" is a will-of-the-wisp. It cannot be located in a single place in an organizational chart. It is the formal responsibility of the President and Congress to establish the legal directives and constraints within which lower-rank officials in the executive branch carry out their work. It is also their responsibility to undertake continuing oversight of their work. Through his

*Because this study is concerned with the President's role as Chief Executive, it will concentrate attention almost entirely upon the problems of managing domestic programs of government. It might be naively assumed that the President should find it easier to manage the domestic problems of America, however intractable the "natives" prove, than to manage problems that required the cooperation of other sovereign nations. In foreign and defense policy, the President has unusual organizational facilities at hand, e.g., the National Security Council and the Central Intelligence Agency; in addition, his authority vis-a-vis subordinates differs, in that he is Commander-in-Chief of the armed forces, and custodian of sovereign prerogatives vis-a-vis foreign nations. These distinctive features do not free the President from worry about the management of foreign and defense policies—but they do make his task different from the domestic policy field. (See e.g., Halperin, 1974; Destler, 1972; Clark and Legere, 1969)

powers of appointment, the President can, subject to Senate confirmation, choose the men responsible for the management of major programs within the executive branch and he can, if he wishes, request the resignation of officials whose choices are inconsistent with his wishes. But this still does not give the President hands-on control of the activities of the executive branch. It only allows him to influence those who themselves, or at yet a further remove, carry out the work done in the name of his Administration. The subordination of bureaucrats establishes distance between them and the President. And distance reduces communication or makes communication more difficult, in circumstances where communication is important as a means of continuing influence. Inevitably, even in the seemingly routine tasks of low-level bureaucrats, there is likely to be some area for discretionary decisions to be made.

Equally important, there is no one particular point in the policy process that can be said to be *most* important. To move from a given political value to a realized government program and, even more, to the desired impact upon society, is a multistep, multiorganization, multiyear process—and influence can be exerted by many different groups, some within government and some outside it, at many points along the way. Schematically, the steps involved in the policy process (cf. Rose, 1973a: 73ff) might look something like the following to an analyst of decision-making:

1. A stimulus to action from events or political groups outside the direct control of a Presidential appointee.
2. Reflection upon the stimulus by a politician in the light of his pre-existing values and predispositions, and those of affected groups, as well as his assessment of the situation at the moment.
3. Announcement of an intention to sponsor some action by government. (If no action is required, then a politician's interest may terminate here, or after the following step).
4. Review of one or more program packages by appropriate policy planning staff within the White House, OMB and appropriate agencies. The review proceeds concurrently with consultations and bargaining with affected interest groups and Congressmen.
5. Announcement of the choice by the President of a particular program alternative.
6. Lobbying to secure necessary Congressional legislation and appropriation to transfer the President's choice into law.
7. If the choice is enacted by Congress, then the program it authorizes must be implemented by operating agencies and line managers. This involves doing many things for the first time, with little or no prior experience of what the consequences will be.
8. Routinization, i.e., the consequences of implementing activities, results in a reasonably predictable or familiar pattern or cycle of

events no longer involving matters of concern to Presidential level staff.

9. Program impact may or may not be of concern to the original sponsors of a measure. The impact of a program is, however, of considerable significance to those who expected to benefit from the program as originally conceived, and to those who are most affected by it, for better or for worse.

An important feature of this or any schematic presentation of the policy process is that it is reversible, and can be entered or left at any point by a politician. One social science approach would assume that politicians formulate political objectives and then see these through to accomplishment by the steps outlined above. Another emphasizes the reactive role of the politician; he does not plan, he copes. This emphasizes the extent to which events force action, including the identification of objectives of an immediate political nature (e.g., to keep people talking to each other) as well as a little longer term (e.g., to get participants to agree about something). But a politician who believes that prudence is the better part of valor may avoid committing himself to political objectives that are controversial because they are topical. He can look instead for government programs that are thought to have a desirable impact, and claim these benefits as his principal political goal. The ambiguity about who is responsible for any given government activity can be an asset for a President wishing to dissociate himself from program failures, and claim credit for successes. The tactic is neatly summed up in John F. Kennedy's alleged remark, a propos a White House sponsored foreign policy choice: "If this works, it will be another triumph of the White House. If it doesn't, it will be another State Department failure."

Inevitably, any schematic outline of policy making oversimplifies; this is the price of setting out succinctly the general properties of a variety of particular events. For example, no explicit reference is made to the role of the courts or of state and local government in the development, choice, and implementation of many federal programs. To outline every program, every expenditure heading, and every organizational activity aggregated in the three tables at the beginning of this chapter would be to lose sight of the forest in the tangled undergrowth of government.

The outline is sufficient for the purpose: to emphasize the complexity of governing. Because of this, much that happens in politics is contingent. The probability of things going wrong, or at least happening different from anticipated, is far greater in Washington, the center of a complex federal system, than in a Greek city-state. Since slips can occur in the management of programs as well as in earlier steps, politicians interested in the impact of their work upon society ignore management questions at their peril. As the epigraph to this chapter notes, even a simple task such as making the trains run on time does not appear easy to manage—especially if you are connected with AMTRAK. So complicated is the task of getting things done in government that Pressman and Wildavsky (1973), the authors of a book called *Implementation* (subtitle: *"Why It's Amazing that Federal Programs Work at All"*), use Rube Goldberg drawings as well as the flow charts of systems analysts to illustrate their view of how government works. Notwithstanding the seeming inanities and circuitous routes of the cartoon devices, it is important to emphasize one thing that government has in common with a device in a Rube Goldberg cartoon: it works.

The question is not whether government works at all, but rather whether government works well or badly. The answer to this question cannot be given in a simple form. For one thing, it depends upon the expectations of an observer. To assume pure rationality in organizational decision making is to prepare oneself for a letdown in Washington. To assume that everything that exists can be justified is to apply the standards of Dr. Pangloss to glorify the Rube Goldberg gadgetry of federal programs, and conclude that "everything is for the best in the best of all possible worlds." Anyone with experience of a large private organization, such as the Bell Telephone Company, whether as customer or employee, may compare the strong points and the pathological features of a private organization with a public one. He will not be predisposed to think that the management of any large organization is an easy task.

The problem facing a President and his appointees, who collectively provide political leadership in the executive branch, is to join choices made in the abstract to concrete actions of government. The more serious among them will be concerned with *effective choice*, that is, giving guidance through choosing goals and objectives, *and* showing sufficient management skill and stamina to make the department move toward them. The management of government programs is less glamorous and less studied than the process by which politicians campaign for office, or make choices as and when elected. A few would argue that the reason for this is that the only goal of politicians is to get re-elected, regarding their office as a sign of status (like membership in the British House of Lords), and not as an obligation to do anything in particular to influence the activities of government. Yet the activities of government go on nonetheless. And the institutions of representative government presuppose that it is through elected officials, especially the President, that Americans can manage, if only a little, to influence the activities of government.

As the following chapter indicates, Presidents have varied in their view of their job—but there is a definite trend through the years in favor of a President who takes charge of government, whatever that phrase may mean. Subsequent chapters explore in detail the difficulties that confront the Presidency in trying to give direction to government. In spite of (or because of) the difficulty of doing this, the management of government remains important. It is the programs as managed by line officials, more than the programs as conceived in the rhetoric of Presidential candidates, that effectively determine what ordinary citizens get from their government.

# 3

# Organizing the Presidency

*In striving together to make our government more efficient, you and I
are taking up in our generation the battle to preserve that freedom of
self-government which our forefathers fought to establish and hand
down to us. They struggled against tyranny, against nonrepresentative
controls, against government by birth, wealth or class, against
sectionalism.*

*Our struggle now is against confusion, against ineffectiveness,
against waste, against inefficiency. This battle, too, must be won, unless
it is to be said that in our generation national self-government broke
down and was frittered away in bad management.*

Franklin D. Roosevelt, 1939

*There shouldn't be a lot of leeway in following the President's policies.
It should be like a corporation, where the executive vice presidents (the
Cabinet officers) are tied closely to the chief executive, or to put it in
extreme terms, when he says jump, they only ask: how high?*

John Ehrlichman, 1972

Every President, consciously or otherwise, depends upon the organizational resources at his disposal to give direction to government. A
President does not govern by doing things himself; he governs by
influencing others to do what he wishes them to do. Some label this
the art of politics, and some the art of management.

Organization is the means by which the views of the man on top
are carried throughout government. It is also the means by which line
managers with knowledge of the day-to-day activities of government
convey this to men whose very eminence makes them remote from
what government is doing at any given moment. Every organization
is an institution for distorting and suppressing as well as transmitting
communications. An elaborate network of filtering procedures is

designed to screen out information that the President does not need to know about activities going on beneath him. Simultaneously, it simplifies and rigidifies the directives coming down from above; only a few dozen officials can be sufficiently close to the President to be familiar with the nuances of a debate leading up to a proclamation of Presidential objectives. Yet if word of the President's wishes is to be conveyed to multitudes of civil servants it must be committed to paper, thus fixing at one point in time the President's public position. Lower echelon officials are left to determine, in the light of their own position, what specifically these objectives mean in the concrete situations confronting them.

Anyone who has ever been at the top of a large organization has at some time suspected that those down below him are not doing what they should be to achieve his objectives, or even, that bureaucrats are ignoring or consciously sabotaging his wishes. Concurrently, the foot soldiers of government, who slog away in government bureaus far from the Presidential limelight, are likely to feel that he is blinded by the glare of publicity, and never sees the problems that they must face every day. The Presidential perspective leads to an approach to organization in terms of control: how can a President get people out in the agencies to do what he wants? The bureaucratic perspective sees the problem in terms of direction: how can a bureaucrat get politicians to state objectives in terms slightly less grandiose than those of Mission Impossible—or how can he get a politician to state objectives in terms that have any operational meaning at all?

Institutions count more than intentions in giving direction to government. They give the wants of a temporarily dominant political coalition durable form, establishing commitments and expectations about government objectives among clients, among Congressmen and among public officials. When writing laws, politicians are very sensitive to the ways in which their decisions about organizational structure can influence the outputs of government agencies, by making them more or less susceptible to pressures from Congress, state and local governments, interest groups, and even from the White House itself. A former senior official in the old Bureau of the Budget describes the political significance of organizations thus:

> Organization structure is one way of expressing national commitment, influencing program direction and ordering priorities. Executive branch structure is in fact a microcosm of American society. Inevitably it reflects the values, conflicts and competing forces to be found in a pluralistic society.
>
> While it may violate some of the canons of scientific management, it does make the government more responsive. (Seidman, 1972: 85)

Consciously or unconsciously, every President must come to
terms with federal government. He does this, not as an organization
theorist or a management consultant, but as a politician. In other
words, he approaches the executive branch thinking about what he
can do with what its institutions offer him.

Upon entering office, a President finds that most of the institutions, like the rooms in the White House, are already fixed, and
alterations run the risk of Congressional outcry and animosity. A
newly elected President is not asked to decide how he wishes to
organize the government, but rather what use he wishes to make of
what is at his disposal. The constitutional inhibitions upon the
President, even if debatable in certain contexts, are nonetheless clear
in structure. Insofar as Presidential objectives require legislation or
appropriations, the President requires the active consent of Congress.
Any action that the President deems to be within his discretion as
Chief Executive is subject to review and conceivably nullification by
the courts, if the President has neither constitutional nor statutory
authority for what he wishes to do.

Most of the institutions of the executive branch are fixed in form
by statute, or can only be altered subject to Congressional approval.
While general responsibility to execute laws rests with the President,
the formal authority to take action is often vested in a Cabinet
Secretary, or in the chief of a particular operating agency. In theory,
the Presidential appointees named to head Cabinet departments and
major federal agencies and to staff positions are there to see that the
President's wishes, insofar as they are clear (and legal), are carried
out by line managers at the operating level. In practice, the relationship between the White House and Presidential appointees out there
in the departments is often strained. Some attribute the failure of
these appointees to personal qualities: "The lines of communication
and control run from the President and his staff to a department
head who sometimes doesn't control his own department and who
most often is a temporary appointee without much knowledge of his
job or experience." (Fortas, 1973: 335) Others attribute the strain to
the tendency of Presidential appointees in operating agencies to
identify with their department's programs, rather than with the
President's. By late 1972 John Ehrlichman no longer was prepared to
rely upon Presidential appointees to act as agents of the White
House: "We only see them at the annual White House Christmas
party; they go off and marry the natives." (Quoted in Nathan, 1975:
40) The President is likely to find that the institutions nominally
underneath him are often outside his reach; the sprawling scale and
size of the executive branch threaten to swamp him, if he ventures to
tread very far into it. As Presidential confidence in his appointees in

the departments declines, he will look for staff closer to him to carry out Presidential objectives.

Within the White House itself, the President has great scope in determining the use he makes of individual members of his White House staff, men whose appointment is personal to himself and not subject to Senate confirmation. He can adapt to his own personal style the direction of men who effectively become his closest assistants. The more a President expands his staff, the more time he must spend as an office manager, supervising the activities that his subordinates undertake. But the President has a limited amount of time that he can devote to supervising his White House staff. The more he expands his staff without supervision, the greater the likelihood that a staff man will, in Franklin D. Roosevelt's phrase, succumb to the temptation to "go into business for himself." Roosevelt avoided this risk by keeping his White House administrative assistants down to half a dozen. When a Roosevelt assistant announced that he needed a man to help him with his work, FDR refused the request, saying that the man was not doing his work properly if he could not do it all himself. Latter-day residents in the White House have run the risk of expanding staff, with results that became evident in the climacteric of Watergate. Congress (unlike some academic writers about the Presidency) has been perennially suspicious of an expanding White House Office. Nonetheless, it has accepted a growth in White House staff from 37 at the start of the second term of Franklin D. Roosevelt to 262 in 1955, and 510 in 1973—plus additional staff carried under other budget headings (see Udall, 1972: 5).

The growth of Councils, Offices and special category officials attached to the Presidency has given the Chief Executive far more staff responsible to himself. Collectively, these groups are lumped together under the heading of the Executive Office of the President. From 1965, under President Johnson, to 1973, under President Nixon, the staff of the Executive Office increased by almost half, from 1576 to 2206. Among these institutions, the Office of Management and Budget (until 1970, the Bureau of the Budget) stands out. With a staff of about 600, it is many times larger than other well known Executive Office units, such as the National Security Council (79) or the Council of Economic Advisers (57). It is the only agency that is concerned with monitoring the whole range of activities within the federal executive. It thus offers a President a unique fund of information derived from continuing review of the whole range of programs of the federal government. Monitoring takes place under the guise of approving budget estimates and regulating the apportionment of funds that Congress appropriates. Budget responsibilities are not seen as an end in themselves, but rather as a means of acquiring detailed knowledge and judgments about the programs being funded.

The career status of the bulk of OMB officials makes the agency a unique repository of knowledge about the ongoing work of government in an environment in which White House advisers change even more frequently than Presidents. OMB staff may even claim to understand many problems of the Presidency better than a newly installed Chief Executive or his White House staff. As part of the Executive Office, they see their role as that of putting their skills at the service of the President. In the words of a former official there: "What drives the staff of the Bureau is its awareness of the appalling scope of a President's job, and of the expectations that crowd in on him. Our role is to supply him with an additional margin of analysis that will make performance of his job possible." (Carey, 1967: 207)

Form follows function. Organization is a tool, not an end in itself. The way in which a President organizes the White House and the Executive Office of the President, the chief communication links between himself and officials in his Administration, tells us much about how he sees the task of giving direction to government. Moreover, the way in which a President sets out to define and carry out any particular objective is greatly influenced by the way in which his administration is organized. Franklin D. Roosevelt consciously sought to avoid the tendency of staff to filter out embarrassing information by creating overlapping and competing channels of communication direct to himself. Dwight D. Eisenhower sought to avoid the tendency of Presidential courtiers to drag the President into their battles by creating a military-type structure to shield the Oval Office from the political facts of life in which Roosevelt gloried.

The debate about how to organize the President's relations with the rest of the executive branch of government is linked to issues far broader than questions of administrative efficiency. The extent to which a President is interested in influencing the organization of government is related to the influence that he wishes to bring to bear upon the world out there beyond his horizon, rimmed as it is by the motley skyline of federal buildings in Washington. A President may start by thinking only of serving a nationwide constituency; this is the constituency that elects him. But if he ignores the organization of influence within the federal executive, then he may find that he has gained popular plaudits for promising to do things, yet lost the ability to direct the only organization through which he can act. As Presidents remain longer in office, they are more likely to turn their minds to organizational reform, in the hope that even if a President cannot achieve the objectives he initially sets for society, at least he can increase his influence within the executive branch itself.

The government of the United States from its foundation until the twentieth century gave very little attention to the question of organizing the Presidency. In 1900 President McKinley had trouble finding someone who wanted to be his secretary. A few years later, a junior reporter from the *Washington Post* wandered through the rooms of the White House looking to see if there was anybody home, until he found the answer by bumping into the ample figure of Theodore Roosevelt in a corridor. The President was not expected to have an organization to carry out his directions, because the Presidency was conceived as a "non-directive" part of government. One reason for this was that government itself was expected to do very little. The idea that the government was responsible for or should somehow direct the affairs of the American people was inconceivable to nearly all who wielded political power for the first century and a half of the nation's life. Insofar as government was meant to act, then the directive power was usually assumed to reside in Congress, the representative assembly of the populace. The Founding Fathers' fear of a central political personage becoming an authoritarian leader —whether on the model of England's incompetent George III, or France's efficient centralizing despot, Louis XIV—led them to divest the executive of many powers that could be derived from a monarchical model. In *The Federalist* No. 70, Alexander Hamilton put the case for a strong President, arguing "energy in the executive is a leading character in the definition of good government." But Hamilton then had to argue that the Presidency, as he conceived it, would be a very different institution from a European monarchy. The President's oath contains a minimalist statement of his duties; he should "faithfully execute the Office of President." It is an oath more suited to an office manager than that of managing director of a large organization.

The rhetoric of the Presidency throughout the nineteenth century exalted Congress as the supreme representative of the populace. James K. Polk recorded the answer he gave to a visiting Oriental, who expressed thanks that he had seen the American King: "There was no King in this country but that he had seen a citizen who had been chosen by the people to manage the government for a limited time." Yet the same Polk not only identified four major objectives at the start of his Administration, he also achieved them. (See Hughes, 1973: 18, 182) Abraham Lincoln never saw his role as that of an office clerk or organization man. A latter-day historian of the Presidency comments, "His frontiersman's conception of the requirements of sound administration were no less naive than Jackson's, whose record as a spoilsman he far surpassed." (Corwin, 1957: 24) Behind the rude exterior and the rhetoric of a man who wished only to serve the Union was the toughness of a politician prepared to use all the resources he could find within government to do what he thought necessary and best, in defiance of Congress, generals, or the Supreme Court.

The Presidents who followed Lincoln, in almost conscious reaction, had a passive vision of the Presidency. Within the newly
established universities, preferences for an active President could be
found. Writing as a Johns Hopkins graduate student, Woodrow
Wilson in the 1880s emphasized the need to centralize power in one
place, and the unsuitability of centralizing power in Congress. Wilson
argued that as the work of government expanded, the administration
of government should be reformed and, by implication, the role of
the Chief Executive strengthened. (Cf. Stillman, 1973: 586f; Ostrom,
1974: 26ff) In the first Administration of William McKinley, Henry
Ford Jones went further in praise of the Presidency; he hailed it as a
revival of "the oldest political institution of the race: the elective
kingsi.ip." (Quoted in Hughes, 1973: 50)

The growth of the federal government from the days of the Civil
War onward made increasingly clear that its affairs could not be
managed by a body constituted like Congress nor, for that matter,
could they be managed by a President approaching his job with no
more knowledge, skill, or hired help than would be needed to run a
New England farm, oversee a Virginia plantation, or clear a prairie
homestead. Some early measures of administrative reform were not
intended to strengthen the directive power of the President. For
example, the 1883 reform of the spoils system in the federal bureaucracy had the incidental effect of reducing the President's
patronage powers, substituting recruitment by civil service examination for appointment by the President on a party patronage basis.
The belief that such reforms were antidemocratic, because they
reduced the responsiveness of career officials to the views of the
popularly elected President of the day, did not die with Andrew
Jackson. Echoes of this sentiment could be heard in the White House
of Richard Nixon.

Other measures of reform were not able to influence management discernibly. For example, Congress established the Cockrell
Committee in 1887 and the Dockery-Cockrell Commission in 1893
to identify mismanagement in government, and to propose improvements. The estimated value of the reforms were slight: a hypothe-
sized saving of less than three per cent of the federal budget at the
time. The principal Congressional achievement, according to a latter-
day commentator, was "shifting the monkey of political responsibility from Congressional to bureaucratic backs." (Mansfield, 1970:
469; see also, Kraines, 1958)

Congressmen came to realize that Congressional government was
itself a cause of the growth of ill-conceived and expanding programs.
As individuals, Congressmen tended to support pork-barrel projects
for their own districts and measures favored by interest groups
supporting them. The President was too weak to assert a general

interest in opposition to the special benefits of pork-barrel legislation. The accumulated cost of sharing out largesse, however, was unpopular with Congressmen in their role as defenders of the public purse. Hence, in the Presidency of William Howard Taft, Congress authorized the White House to investigate ways to promote economy and efficiency in government. Woodrow Wilson's Presidency, by the stimulus given to domestic activities as well as the exigencies of managing a war effort, increased concern about the adequacies of historic institutions to meet the problems of the time. A respected Republican, Dr. Nicholas Murray Butler, told a Congressional Committee at the end of World War I:

> As I read our political and governmental history, we have patched and amended our administrative machinery to meet emergencies and conditions for about 125 years, but we have never really taken up the question of its reorganization from the standpoint of the governmental needs and business methods of today, when our federal government has become, of course, the largest business undertaking in the world. My fundamental proposition is that all over the world we are faced by the question of the breakdown of governments as efficient agents, their breakdown, I mean, before public opinion. (Quoted in Marx, 1945: 667)

In 1921 this concern resulted in the creation of the Bureau of the Budget, an organization charged with receiving departmental estimates for appropriations and reviewing them on behalf of the President, so that a single budget could be presented from the executive branch for Congressional consideration. Congress saw the Bureau of the Budget as an agency that would, with all the authority of the President behind it, restrain agencies that wanted separately more than it was collectively good that the country should spend. In order to do this, the Bureau of the Budget, although nominally located in the Treasury Department, was given powers to delve into the management of programs in a way hitherto unprecedented in the federal executive. Its first director, General Charles Dawes, invoked an idea that John Ehrlichman also voiced. Addressing an initial meeting of leading executive branch officials in 1921, he sought to "emphasize in the mind of every man there his relation to the President as head of a business organization." (Dawes, 1923: 8)

The President who received this organizational asset was Warren G. Harding. Harding, however, wanted less rather than more advice. He once bemoaned his White House job thus: "I listen to one side and they seem right, and then I talk to the other side and they seem just as right, and there I am where I started . . . God, what a job!" (Quoted in Sorensen, 1963: 42) Following Harding's death, the Bureau of the Budget became a servant of Calvin Coolidge. Coolidge too believed in a nondirective Presidency. He summed up his passive philosophy thus: "If you see ten troubles coming down the road, you can be sure that nine will run into the ditch before they reach you, and you have to battle with only one." (Quoted in Hughes 1973: 97) The Bureau of the Budget was left in the unhappy position of being the institutional eyes and ears of an organization that had no active head. The Bureau concentrated on the task that Congressmen originally had in mind: enforcing savings upon federal agencies, not only down to the last penny, but also, down to the last fraction of a penny. While Herbert Hoover brought to the White House a great concern with organization and detail, Hoover lacked the vision to identify goals that would attract political support sufficient to give positive direction to government.

The entry of Franklin D. Roosevelt to the White House brought an end to the nondirective Presidency. But Roosevelt's style of political leadership was not that of formal command, as in a military hierarchy, nor did he identify objectives and allocate resources to clearly prescribed ends, as in an economist's model of organizational decision making. Roosevelt's method of leadership was more subtle; it was indirect leadership. Roosevelt preferred the fox's circuitous approach to problems, rather than the forceful dramatic rush forward of a lion, fearful in countenance—until he falls into a trap. A major feature of Roosevelt's style was the avoidance of early or explicit identification of objectives. Instead, he encouraged a multiplicity of executive branch officials to investigate, and even act regarding pressing problems. Then he would decide, in the light of what their experience revealed, on any commitments he wished to make himself. In order to divest himself of responsibility for what did not work, the President needed to keep the ties between him and his Administration loose rather than tie subordinates closely to him, as in John Ehrlichman's model of the Presidency. A Cabinet officer sponsoring a bill that he thought expressed the President's objectives sometimes had a disconcerting response from the White House, when he found himself in trouble in Congress. "It is all your trouble, not mine," he once informed his Cabinet officers with reference to the bills that they were sponsoring. This was his attitude toward departmental operations generally, always excepting those things that he wanted for his own. (Neustadt, 1963: 856)

To gain the organizational resources he desired to give direction to government, in 1936 Roosevelt appointed a Committee on Administrative Management, consisting of three eminent scholars of public administration. Louis Brownlow was its head. The Committee's Report invoked patriotism: "The forward march of American democracy at this point of our history depends more upon effective

management than upon any other single factor" (1937: 53); biparti-
sanship, citing a Republican and two anti-Roosevelt Democrats as
pioneers in improving management in government: Governor Frank
Lowden of Illinois, Governor Al Smith of New York, and Governor
(later Senator) Harry F. Byrd of Virginia (p. 3); and scientific authority: "Fortunately the foundations of effective management in public
affairs no less than in private are well known." (p. 3) Conscious of
the critics of the growth of Presidential power, the Committee
argued: "Our choice is not between power and no power, but
between responsible but capable popular government and irrespon-
sible autocracy . . . only a treasonable design could oppose careful
attention to the best and soundest practice of government." (pp. 2,
53) To ensure that "the blessings of liberty" could continue to be
provided the American people, the Committee made recommendations under five headings: the expansion of the White House Staff;
the development of a group of managerial agencies concerned with
the whole of the executive branch under Presidential aegis; the
extension of the merit system; the reorganization of the departments
and agencies of the executive branch; and the improvement of fiscal
audit and accountability procedures.

Roosevelt welcomed the Committee's not unexpected endorsement of his own desire to enhance the institutions of the Presidency.
As an epigraph to this chapter shows, he too was ready to use an
appeal to the Founding Fathers to strengthen his argument for
"energizing" the executive branch by White House initiators. The
President submitted the Committee's recommendations to Congress
with the confession that "it is humanly impossible, under the system
which we have, for him fully to carry out his constitutional duty as
Chief Executive . . . to co-ordinate and manage the departments and
activities in accordance with the laws enacted by Congress." (p. iv)

If the administrative optimism of the 1930s sounds curiously old
fashioned today, there is nonetheless contemporary significance in
what followed. The most famous sentence in the Report is the
statement, "The President needs help." To provide this, the Committee recommended the provision of executive assistants to act as
aides in dealing with the federal agencies. What is often overlooked is
that the Committee on Administrative Management (1937: 5)
emphasized that their number should be small, "probably not ex-
ceeding six in number." Moreover, "they would not be interposed
between the President and the heads of his departments; they would
not be assistant presidents in any sense." The President managed to
get his aides, and an Executive Office of the President with a Bureau
of the Budget with a staff of forty-five. But the grander ambitions of
the Committee for reorganizing the Presidency floundered on the
familiar reef of Congressional opposition. (See Mansfield, 1970:

478ff) To remind the President of the limitations of his resources, Congress killed the Presidentially reformulated National Resources Planning Board, a body that the Brownlow Committee had seen as the prototype of a policy planning unit for the White House. The achievement of the Brownlow Committee was as much conceptual as institutional. Henceforth, the responsibilities of the Chief Executive have been seen less in terms of saving money and more in terms of broader political questions of the most effective organizational means of "getting things done that we, the American people, want done." (p. 1)

In wartime the pressure for results was enormously magnified. The mobilization of economic resources for the war effort and the management of those resources by the President, as Commander-in-Chief as well as Chief Executive, threw up gigantic problems. On the domestic front Roosevelt continued his practice of indirect leadership through competitive delegation of Presidential responsibilities. The war greatly strengthened the Bureau of the Budget so recently established as part of the Executive Office of the President. It became responsible for the organization of many new units required by the war effort. The inevitable problems that arose in the management of agencies and in the resolution of disputes between agencies provided a justification for the work of the Bureau's Division of Administrative Management. (Marx, 1945: 888ff) The Director of the Bureau from 1939 to 1946, Harold B. Smith, emphasized the Bureau's managerial rather than its fiscal role. Shortly after assuming office he defined its task as "to serve as agent of the President in his job of management and to help execute whatever program or policy the Administrative may have undertaken." (Quoted in Pearson, 1943: 129) Yet Smith was no simpleminded crusader for management efficiency. He went out of his way to emphasize "the weakness of management . . . its tendency to lose sight of major objectives." (1945: 33) He attributed this to an overemphasis on matters of form and procedure, and the neglect of the substance. By the end of the war, the Bureau of the Budget had grown from a staff of 45 to 564.

In the aftermath of World War II, Harry Truman and Dwight D. Eisenhower, each in his own way, helped consolidate the organizational upheaval that had occurred in Washington in the Roosevelt years. Truman cast himself in the role of an activist President, ready to take decisions—even though he found it more difficult to achieve objectives identified for domestic policy than those identified in international affairs. Like his predecessor, Truman had a small White House staff, and chaired morning staff meetings himself. He showed a greater respect than Roosevelt for the separation of powers within the executive branch; he expected the Bureau of the Budget to do staff work for him as career officials in the Executive Office of the

President, while he himself made the decisions that were constitutionally and politically the responsibility of the President. Dwight D. Eisenhower further consolidated earlier changes by demonstrating that even a Republican with as conservative and *laissez faire* an attitude as his own could not reduce the level of federal government activity to that found in the 1920s decade of normalcy. In fact President Eisenhower could not even hold public expenditure to the level it was at in the final year of the Truman Administration. In 1952, the federal government's gross expenditure was $99.8 billion; in 1960, it was $151.3 billion. (Mosher and Poland, 1964: 155) Organizationally, Eisenhower's chief innovation at the White House was the establishment of a military-type staff reporting system, with most communications funnelled to him or disposed of at this penultimate point in the hierarchy by the assistant to the President from 1953 to 1958, Sherman Adams.

Both Truman and Eisenhower gave former President Herbert Hoover a commission to review the organization of the executive branch, and make recommendations for improvement. The first Hoover Commission, sitting from 1947 to 1949, was a bow by a Democratic President facing a Republican Congress. Ex-President Hoover turned to businessmen and management consultant firms to evaluate what was wrong with the executive branch, and how it could be set right. As an ex-President, he favored a strong executive branch and, within it, concentrating both power and responsibility in the hands of the Chief Executive: "Responsibility and accountability are impossible without authority—the power to direct. The exercise of authority is impossible without a clear line of command from the top to bottom, and a return line of responsibility and accountability from the bottom to the top." (Hoover Commission, 1949: 1) One latter-day commentator notes, "The Commission's reports, which avoided like poison any mention of the Brownlow Committee, made the doctrines of that Committee orthodox." (Mansfield, 1970: 483) As a Republican, Hoover favored cuts in substantive programs as the most effective way to achieve fiscal economy, which he valued as an eventual goal of reorganization efforts. But the Commission was vague in detailing which programs should be axed—and the re-election of President Truman in 1948 meant an effective end to talk of saving money. The second Hoover Commission of 1953-1955 was launched at the start of a Republican Administration. But by the time the Commission reported in 1955 President Eisenhower had had his fill of administrative reorganization, including notably, the elevation of high-spending programs in health, education and welfare to Cabinet status. And ex-President Hoover had had his fill of self-restraint; the second Commission's recommendation to reform by cutting back heavily the role of the federal government was ignored.

The Bureau of the Budget's efforts to improve management went into decline in this period. In July, 1949, President Truman issued an executive order directing the head of each agency to review management procedures and report periodically to the Bureau on its progress. But the meetings, initially chaired by the President himself, came to nothing. Management improvement tended to be treated as something apart from the major work of the departments and, by being isolated, lacked impact within the departments and interest from politicians. In the words of one public administration expert, the management improvement program "started a flow of paper from management analysts in the agencies to the Bureau that proved to be essentially worthless in meeting the objective of stimulating aggressive efforts to improve administrative management." (Bernstein, 1970: 507) The number of staff assigned to management tasks in the Bureau of the Budget declined from about fifty-five professionals in 1948 to twenty-nine in 1960. Morale also declined, with the loss of the crusading confidence that public administration experts had brought to Washington in the 1930s. In the words of one scholar, "Many public administrators came away from their wartime experiences rejecting the administrative dogmas that had been handed down to them, and disengagement from practical administrative affairs became a widespread means of accommodation to their own uncertainties." (Schick, 1970: 530) In reaction against this record, a Committee chaired by Nelson Rockefeller recommended to the President the abolition of the Bureau of the Budget, because of its alleged narrow fixation upon budgeting procedures, and the creation of a new Office of Executive Management under the President's aegis, to stimulate a more positive approach to program design and policy planning by staff of the Executive Office of the President. (See Rockefeller, 1965: 174ff)

Since the election of John F. Kennedy, the White House has been in the hands of activist Presidents. While operating in different ways, each incumbent has been concerned with going deeper into the activities of the departments of the executive branch. The principal motive force has been political—the desire of the President of the day to have greater influence upon the actions of his Administration. The movement has been across the board, affecting questions of choice as well as management concerns. The desire of the President to intervene more does not give him more hours in the week in which to act effectively. To extend his influence, the President has had to expand his staff within the White House and the Executive Office. Moreover, a declaration of will and intent has not eliminated the organizational problems that faced his predecessors.

The moral that could be drawn from a succession of activist Presidents has been provided by the most active of their number,

Lyndon Johnson (1964: 147): "The Presidency is a much tougher job from the inside than I thought it was from the outside." The difficulty arises in part from the burden of responsibility and the liability for blame that rests uniquely upon the President, rather than being dispersed through a number of ministers in a Cabinet-cum-parliamentary system of government. It also arises from the intractability of many of the problems—an intractability more apparent to an incumbent than to a candidate. John F. Kennedy (1962: 134) reflected upon the difference in perspective thus: "In the first place the problems are more difficult than I had imagined they were. Secondly, there is a limitation upon the ability of the United States to solve these problems." As if these problems were not enough, Presidents have also found themselves repeatedly frustrated in trying to cope with what should notionally be the least of their problems: the management of the executive branch of government. In the words of an anonymous former White House staff man, "The greatest difficulty we had was getting things out of the executive agencies. . . . Requests get lost among the bureaucracy and it is so tough to penetrate all their crap." (Cronin, 1970: 585)

In defense and foreign affairs, the major focus of political interest in John F. Kennedy's Presidency, organizational questions were perceived as important because of what could happen through mismanagement. The abortive 1961 invasion of the Bay of Pigs, endorsed by the new President on the basis of advice coming up through channels, was interpreted in the White House as evidence of the need to organize very carefully the way in which a President approached a major foreign policy decision. The Cuban missile crisis of 1962 gave the President an unexpectedly prompt and grave opportunity to put these lessons into effect. The White House handling of the second Cuban crisis was undoubtedly successful in achieving the intended objective. The lessons that can be drawn from it about the "essentials" of governing are less clear. (See Allison, 1971)

The White House brought in a management expert (and ex-Harvard Business School professor), Robert McNamara, to head the Department of Defense. The "organizational revolution" at the Pentagon enhanced Secretary Robert McNamara's status in the White House. The changes primarily involved departmental reorganization: they were not a matter of White House action. The adoption of new analytic techniques in the Office of the Secretary enhanced both the Secretary's and the President's ability to see the big picture and to reckon more precisely the advantages and disadvantages of program alternatives. Incidentally, it strengthened belief that the federal bureaucracy was manageable—if only the right man or methods could be found.

In domestic policy, Kennedy felt hamstrung by his minute electoral majority. His motto was: "The President can't administer a department, but at least he can be a stimulant." (Hirschfield, 1973: 137) White House assistants had no doubt that continuing stimulus was needed from them. A few years later Arthur Schlesinger, Jr. (1965: 592) recalled:

> *Wherever we have gone wrong—from Cuba to fiscal policy—has been because we have not had sufficient confidence in the New Frontier approach to impose it on the government. Every important mistake has been the consequence of excessive deference to the permanent government. In too many areas we have behaved as the Eisenhower administration would have behaved. The problem of moving forward seemed in great part the problem of making the permanent government responsive to the policies of the presidential government.*

The Johnson White House gave first priority to the President's choice of proposals to recommend to Congress for legislative enactment. The State of the Union message and all that flowed into it and from it became the action-forcing process that drove White House staff concern with matters of domestic policy. The most significant institutional innovation of the Johnson White House was the creation of task forces to identify issues that might justify a Presidential recommendation for new legislation. Under Truman and Eisenhower the great bulk of the President's legislative program had been based upon departmental recommendations, filtered through the Bureau of the Budget, and vetted by the White House at the final stage of compiling the State of the Union address itself. (See Neustadt, 1954, 1955) Kennedy had used task forces to suggest initiatives in the period between his election and inauguration, but not systematically. Thereafter, under Lyndon Johnson, Bill Moyers and then Joseph Califano became responsible for a small staff that took the initiative in the White House to seek out program objectives and prepare legislation recommendations consistent with the President's preferences. (See Thomas and Wolman, 1969; Anderson, 1968: 352ff)

Concern with legislative objectives permeated the whole year in the Johnson White House. The cycle commenced in March or April, after the special messages of the previous State of the Union message had become primarily a problem of lobbying support on the Hill. Califano began to compile an ideas book containing suggestions from many sources—the President, White House staff, the departments, and outsiders. For example, the 516-page 1968 ideas book included more than 100 possible topics. A five-man staff was then responsible for organizing task forces to investigate the most interesting ideas in more detail. Members of task forces came from outside government as well as from inside the executive branch. Departments were notified of task forces concerning their responsibilities, and were invited to nominate individuals who might appropriately serve. Departmental nominees were not included as of right, but only on the basis of individual reputation. After a first confused year, each task force also included an official from the Bureau of the Budget to provide cost estimates as discussions progressed and, when task force recommendations involved significant expenditures, to make a group indicate relative priorities related to sums that might be available in the forthcoming budget. In September and October, the task forces winnowed down many ideas to about two dozen potential Presidential objectives for legislative action. By this stage, the January deadline of the State of the Union message was prompting the President to monitor their work more closely. Major proposals were sent out to the departments for comment. Concurrently, Califano and the Director of the Bureau of the Budget began to consider the implications of possible new objectives for the forthcoming year's budget. By December, the President received option papers from his own staff. He could then choose to endorse, discard, or delay a choice of objectives defined by an unprecedented amount of White House staff work.

The most far-reaching and significant attempt of the Johnson Administration to get on top of the activities of the executive branch came from the introduction of the Planning Programming Budgeting System (PPBS) in 1965. The President personally announced the introduction of PPBS in the hope that it would provide a better way of identifying political objectives, and relating them to Presidential budget choices between alternative programs intended to reach desired ends. PPBS was intended to increase the efficiency with which programs were selected and launched in the expansionist climate of the Great Society. The new men of PPBS defined their role thus:

> The central issue is, of course, nothing less than the definition of the ultimate objectives of the federal government as they are realized through operational decisions. Set in this framework, the designation of a schedule of programs may be described as building a bridge between a matter of political philosophy (what is government for?) and the administrative function of assigning scarce resources among alternative governmental objectives. The unique function of a program budget is to implement the conclusions of a political philosophy through the assignment of resources to their accomplishment.
>
> In a number of areas no clear objectives have ever been laid down. This undesirable condition has prevailed in the field of international aid and investment, but it can also be found in many domestic areas including, among others, agriculture, transportation, education, and unemployment. (Anshen, 1966)

PPBS failed. The true believer, like any religious enthusiast, can claim that it failed because it was never properly implemented. The more usual explanation is that it failed because it promised to do too much. (Merewitz and Sosnick, 1971; Lyden and Miller, 1972). PPBS left behind a significant legacy. Many economists brought to Washington to implement PPBS in domestic agencies have learned the ways of the city well enough to survive the failure of one technique, and found positions in operating departments, particularly staff jobs advising the Secretary. Their characteristic point of view—a concentration upon what programs will buy—raises questions about the objectives of government. Like the Califano task forces, such economists are not professionally concerned with what happens, once choices are enacted into law.

The very success of President Johnson in achieving his chief objective—Congressional enactment of Great Society legislation—was followed by disillusionment in Washington and in the field, as the new programs revealed the shortcomings of program management and, even worse, the unmanageability of programs designed with little regard for how they might be implemented. Part of the failure arose from the unrealistically grand objectives of the programs. In the words of two sympathetic critics, Ginzberg and Solow (1974: 213):

> *The mid-1960s saw the President, his advisers and the Congressional leadership wantonly blur the distinction between campaign promises and legislative commitments. From one point of view, the Great Society programs were doomed from the moment of their enactment. There was no prospect that any government could deliver on such ambitious promises.*

As the difficulties of carrying out Great Society programs became more prominent, in November, 1966 President Johnson appointed a task force on government organization, to recommend actions to improve the direction of government. The task force was chaired by a friend of the President, Ben W. Heineman, a Chicago railroad executive. Its members were familiar with viewing government from the President's perspective, for they were: the Director of the Bureau of the Budget, the Secretary of Defense, three former Executive Office officials, McGeorge Bundy, Kermit Gordon and William Capron, and one academic, Herbert Kaufman of Yale. The Heineman task force (1967: 1) diagnosed the White House problem thus:

> *Many domestic social programs are under severe attack.* Some criticism is political. *It comes from those who oppose the goals of these national programs.* Some criticism stems from deflated hopes, *with current funding levels well below ultimate need and demand.* Some criticism

arises because of alleged organizational and managerial weaknesses. *After several months of study, we believe the organizational criticism is merited. [Emphasis in the original]*

The task force recommended that the President create an Office of Program Development to provide a unit within the Executive Office concerned with the definition of legislative and administrative objectives and programs. In addition, it recommended the creation of an Office of Program Co-ordination to handle the interagency and intergovernmental conflicts that often gave government programs their reputation for being badly managed or lacking any central direction. To dramatize the need for linking program choice with program actions, Heineman recommended that the name of the Bureau of the Budget (the chief agency affected) be changed to the Bureau of Program Development and Management.

In the aftermath of Watergate it is tempting to dismiss President Nixon's White House in a phrase adapted from Walter Bagehot's description of the government of England's George III: "a veritable museum exhibit of the defects of a Constitutional monarch." It is easy to forget that while the Nixon Presidency created many problems, the Presidency that Richard Nixon inherited on January 20, 1969, was already an institution with many problems. A budget director for Kennedy and Johnson, Kermit Gordon, defined the central theme as something worse than an inability to give positive direction to government; it was an inability even to react in a positive and purposeful manner: "the government's losing struggle to cope with the crisis of convulsive change in which we live." (Quoted in Seidman, 1972: 87)

Symptoms of dissatisfaction and demands for change came from persons of many different political outlooks. The Heineman Commission (1967: 2) criticized the agencies and units responsible for carrying out the Great Society as "a collection of fragmented bureau fiefdoms." Robert Wood (1970: 95) a former Secretary and Under-Secretary at HUD under Johnson, criticized White House staff for letting minor problems squeeze out major ones in a vain attempt to "subdue outlying bureaucracies" while "policy-making emerges at the bottom." A Bureau of the Budget (1967) internal staff review reflected critical self-doubt by asking: "What business are we in? What business should we be in? What sort of Bureau should we have?" A retiring assistant director of the Bureau of the Budget, William Carey (1969), identified White House weaknesses as: a shortage of policy analysis; poor communications within the executive branch and with public and Congressional opinion; a lack of outreach beyond that of Cabinet officers and a limited group of presidential appointees, and thus an overall weakening of the command

and control capability of the White House. During the 1968 campaign, Presidential aspirants such as Hubert Humphrey and Nelson Rockefeller urged major changes in the institutions of the Presidency (Cronin and Greenberg, 1969: 312ff), echoing earlier pleas made by Dwight D. Eisenhower and on behalf of Lyndon Johnson (Jackson, 1965: 198). The winner, Richard Nixon, was to show by his actions that he desired the biggest changes of all.

The political thrust of the Nixon Presidency was consistent in intent, although shifting in the particular methods employed by the President and those acting in his name, such as John Ehrlichman and Robert Haldeman. Moreover, many of the basic operating assumptions had been endorsed by those who had served his predecessors at the White House. The President and his staff saw themselves as the only representatives of the general interest in Washington, because only the President was elected by a nationwide constituency. The mandate doctrine could be invoked in almost any context, immediately after Nixon's overwhelming victory in the 1972 presidential election. The simple retort of a Presidential speechwriter to accusations of illegal White House activities was, according to Bernstein and Woodward (1975: 316): "61 per cent." McGeorge Bundy (1968: 378), as well as John Ehrlichman, endorsed the view that Cabinet officers should be tied in to the White House, acting under Presidential direction as well as Presidential grants of authority. The assumption that accountability in the executive branch required a clear line of command from top to bottom can be found in the Brownlow report and in the Hoover Commission; it justified executive reorganizations from 1969 to 1973. Many (although not all) changes followed recommendations of leading scholars in public administration, as a panel report from the National Academy of Public Administration to Senator Ervin's Committee noted. (Mosher et al., 1974: 9)

Consisting primarily of men new to Washington, the Nixon staff suspected that civil servants appointed and promoted by Democratic predecessors would be out of sympathy with Republican objectives, and slow to carry out Presidential wishes. The staff was correct in its assumption about the political values of senior Washington officials, according to a survey of 126 supergrade and executive level appointees undertaken by University of Michigan scholars in 1970. The researchers found "a career bureaucracy ideologically hostile to many of the directions pursued by the Nixon administration in the realm of social policy." (Aberbach and Rockman, 1974: 30) They said that their interviews support the quip, "Even paranoids may have real enemies." White House staff jumped to the conclusion that career officials who had bent their efforts to work for Democratic

Presidents could not or would not do the same for them. The men supposed to give direction to the bureaucracy became antibureaucratic in their outlook. Complaints of bureaucratic unresponsiveness are nothing new. Ron Zeigler's charge—"I have seen in the last few years that occasionally the bureaucracy is not as responsive to the White House as some may suspect"—is a mild version of Arthur Schlesinger's complaint—"The problem of moving forward seemed in great part the problem of making the permanent government responsive to the policies of the Presidential government." (Cf. Seidman, 1972: 83 and Schlesinger, 1965: 592)

The basic political strategy of the Nixon White House is aptly described as the creation of an Administrative Presidency, determining and carrying out policies through administrative powers vested in (or claimed to rest in) the President. While every modern President has made use of administrative powers as often as he could, the Nixon White House was unique in relying solely upon them. The President could not expect to achieve legislative success from a Democratic Congress as Lyndon Johnson had done. Nor did the President wish to be known by the legislation enacted during his tenure in office. As a Republican, his bias was to *reduce* the government's role in domestic policy; hence, negative powers were often sufficient for his objectives. Through the veto power, impoundment, purging and harassing career officials, and in novel interpretations of implied powers and prerogatives that were not always accepted by the courts (for a detailed catalog see Schlesinger's 1974 re-thinking of the liabilities of "The Imperial Presidency"), the Nixon White House explored how it could get its hands on the operations of government. The strategy assumed, not without some justification, that "operations is policy." (Nathan, 1975: 62) Questions of the management and the reorganization of government became invested with far more political significance—both to the President and his opponents—than at any time since Franklin D. Roosevelt's second term.

The President's most ambitious reorganization proposal was prepared early in his first term by an Advisory Council on Executive Organization headed by a businessman successful in creating a huge conglomerate company, Roy Ash. Ash's maxim was: "Organization is policy." In a 400-page report presented in 1970 this council of businessmen and management experts proposed a comprehensive and fundamental reorganization of the departments of the executive branch. President Nixon justified the upheaval in the language of functionalism, that is, the need to fit institutions to objectives:

> We sometimes seem to have forgotten that government is not in
> business to deal with subjects on a chart but to achieve real objectives
> for real human beings. These objectives will never be fully achieved

*unless we change our old ways of thinking. It is not enough merely to reshuffle departments for the sake of reshuffling them. We must rebuild the executive branch according to a new understanding of how government can best be organized to perform effectively.*

*The key to that new understanding is the concept that the executive branch of the government should be organized around basic goals. (Presidential message to Congress of March 25, 1971)*

The President failed in his attempt to get Congressional approval of this grand reorganization plan to transform the seven domestic Cabinet departments principally concerned.

The President did succeed in creating a Domestic Council under White House control to provide the President with program planning and monitoring. (See Kessel, 1975) The Domestic Council had a large staff by Executive Office standards, about two dozen professionals. It also had direct political access to the President, since John Ehrlichman was its executive director. The idea of a White House agency to prepare policy options for the President was not original. Nelson Rockefeller, Hubert Humphrey, and the Heineman commission, among others, had all endorsed such an institution, and Joseph Califano's task force team informally undertook this work with a much smaller staff. Nor was there anything novel in Domestic Council staff intervening on behalf of the White House in the direction and management of activities of executive branch agencies. Roy Ash bluntly described the situation as one in which "the formal structure shows no supervision of these many departments and activities, and the informal structure looks to the White House staff to perform that immediate supervision." In such circumstances, the President has "a limited number of alternatives. One of them is to ignore those departments and activities completely. Another one is to add to his White House staff." The Domestic Council had the National Security Council as its prototype. But there was one fatal difference. The NSC advises the President about matters that he can promptly act upon. The President's unchallenged prerogative powers as Commander-in-Chief and Chief of State ensure compliance from the Departments of Defense and State. The sprawling and heterogeneous agencies of domestic policy are not similarly tied to the White House, nor can the President claim to be their Commander-in-Chief. Domestic agencies derive their authority from public laws and appropriations passed by Congress.

Concurrently with creating the Domestic Council to prepare new policy choices, President Nixon reorganized the Bureau of the Budget in the hope of strengthening the management of continuing government programs. The President's reorganization message of March 12, 1970 spoke of a fundamental shift in the agency's work: "preparation of the budget as such will no longer be its dominant overriding concern." Instead, the renamed institution was to emphasize management. The word Budget was only inserted into the title of the restyled Office of Management and Budget at the insistence of Congress. The President recommended that OMB improve government management through the evaluation of program performance, the improvement of interagency field cooperation, the development of information systems, the development of career executive talent, the recruitment and training of executive talent through the Civil Service Commission, and also, continuing the Bureau's legislative reference and statistical coordination activities. The recommendations were familiar prescriptions of optimistic and progressive reformers of the federal bureaucracy.

Following his November, 1972 election triumph, President Nixon initiated yet another reorganization. The object of hands-on control of management was retained, but the means of securing control altered: it was to move White House staff out to the agencies. The President named trusted White House staff to become heads of Cabinet departments, or to occupy sensitive staff supervisory positions just below departmental Secretaries. It was hoped that men loyal to the President would be able to move departments into line with White House objectives from their position within the agencies, as they had been unable to do from the outside, that is, from posts in the White House. The best known figure to shift was Henry Kissinger, who became Secretary of State. The reorganization scheme divided responsibilities for policy among five Presidential appointees: Robert Haldeman, John Ehrlichman, Roy Ash, Henry Kissinger, and George P. Shultz, then Secretary of the Treasury. James T. Lynn, Earl Butz, and Caspar Weinberger were also expected to coordinate policies of several Cabinet departments. The new division of responsibilities, according to Roy Ash, was intended to avoid Presidential involvement in management issues. "This hierarchical form does allow pushing down authority and responsibility out of the President's office. It does allow more and more of these interagency issues to be dealt with outside of the President's office. That's the whole purpose of the reorganizational change." (Bonafede, 1973: 335)

The reorganization efforts of the Nixon Presidency were greeted with scepticism and disfavor by many hands in Washington. A survey of federal program managers taken by OMB in late 1971 found that three-fourths could see little difference between their dealings with the old Budget Bureau and the management-oriented OMB. An ex-Budget official told the *National Journal* (Mullaney, 1971: 2378), "I don't know of any President who has been able to control the bureaucracy. Rhetoric aside, every President said he was going to do it and no President ever has."

One cause of negative reaction was the belief that management is "Mickey Mouse" stuff. The Nixon staff were aware of this feeling; they countered by arguing that good management meant far more than neat organization charts and personnel files. Fred Malek (1971: 12) spoke thus of his initial experience as a Harvard Business School graduate in Washington: "I soon learned that when most people spoke of 'management' they were really referring to administrative or housekeeping activities. They were not referring to a broader range of functions such as setting goals, motivating and directing subordinates and assessing performance—activities which I have always considered the essence of management." A second source of antagonism within OMB was that the Nixon changes introduced additional levels of political appointees. OMB was physically split in three layers; the Director, in his role as a Presidential adviser, had an office in the West Wing of the White House; top political echelons were in the Old Executive Office Building; and career officials in the New Executive Office Building on the other side of Pennsylvania Avenue. Some OMB career staff sought to bridge the gap, by offering their information to White House staff in return for the prestige of working closer to the President. Their success led colleagues to accuse them of becoming "White House happy," abandoning professional detachment to become uncritical promoters of White House ideas. In principle, there was nothing new in Budget underlings working directly to the White House; the practice had been going on at least since Truman's time. (Neustadt, 1955: 620) Like senior English civil servants, Budget officials saw themselves remaining "professional" in highly political surroundings. (See Heclo, 1975) President Nixon's team did not appreciate the distinction that was important to the morale of the veterans of the Budget. It preferred to deal with new men, whom it thought of as its own men.

The organizational changes of the Nixon Presidency assumed that problems of choice and problems of management could not be divorced from one another. The men with their hands on the action in the operating agencies had demonstrated that they could do (or refuse to do) what the White House wanted. Yet the President had also concluded that the burdens of monitoring and guiding government in its continuing operations were not for him. He wished to save himself for great questions of choice, especially in foreign affairs, a field he had always preferred to domestic policy. Thus, he was ready to delegate vast *de facto* powers to those whom he believed were loyal to him, because they were dependent upon his power of appointment. The effort of reform was justified, in the eyes of those involved, by the prizes that could be won. In the words of Harvard Professor Richard Neustadt, an adviser of Democratic Presidents: "All this is a determined effort to get control of the details and operations of the executive establishment. Mr. Nixon is not the first President who wanted to do this. However, his is the most intensive effort that I can recall. My guess is the President, like all of his predecessors, will be disappointed by the results." (Quoted in Bonafede, 1973: 339)

The desire of the Nixon White House to create a "monocracy ruled from the top through a strictly disciplined hierarchical system" (Mosher et al., 1974: 11) became, in the words of a former Executive Office adviser, "The Plot that Failed." (Nathan, 1975) The reforms were not proven to be unworkable—though there were many in Washington ready to argue that. They collapsed because of the serio-comic inadequacies of the White House plumbers unit and the persistent probing of a small number of men who feared that the plans of the Nixon White House to take over things extended far beyond the powers of the Presidency as lawfully construed.

The fall of the Nixon White House does not tell us whether the plans of the President should have succeeded. The question is: was this the right method to govern contemporary America. A panel of public administrators advised Senator Ervin's Committee that the answer is "No.""The American state then would have approached a monocracy, ruled from the top through a strictly disciplined hierarchical system. It would have become difficult to pin responsibility for decisions or actions upon anyone short of the top man, and he was, for the most part, inaccessible and unaccountable . . . (except for) electoral defeat or impeachment." (Mosher et al., 1974: 11) Robert Nathan (1975: 92) argues that, if scholars of the President would only set aside their dislike of Richard Nixon and their Democratic Party allegiance, they would recall that they have long favored a strong (even an Imperial) Presidency. The goal of the monocratic Presidency was to provide "a force to counter entrenched domestic-program bureaucracies and interest groups" and permit the return of power "to the give-and-take of democratic political processes," as embodied in the decisions of an elected Chief Executive. Peter Woll and Rochelle Jones (1973: 183f) endorse the Nixon view that "the federal bureaucracy puts important limits on the power of the President . . . because it has independent sources of political power." But they conclude that a "semi-autonomous bureaucracy," although often inefficient and yielding to special interest group pressure, helps to preserve the balance of powers among the branches of government that is necessary for the preservation of our system of constitutional democracy."

The problems of managing the executive branch did not leave Washington with the departure of Richard Nixon. They are alive and well in the Washington of Gerald R. Ford. There is every sign that President Ford is in agreement with his immediate predecessor about the nature of the problems facing a contemporary Presidency. The first assumption in common is that the White House should play an active part in the direction of the work of the executive branch. Secondly, it is assumed that this requires the President to assemble a sizeable staff of personal advisers. Thirdly, White House staff are inclined to believe that the management of government leaves something to be desired in terms of program effectiveness and political responsiveness to the directions of the President. The White House optimists think that the problems are political: the departments will not respond to persuasion or commands because there are more powerful competing pressures. The less sanguine fear that the problem is intrinsic in the structure of bureaucracy. The most pessimistic are those who fear that the optimists and disenchanted are both right in their diagnosis of the President's difficulties.

The exigencies of repudiating the past as well as Ford's own Congressional background are likely to emphasize a different White House style than that flourishing from 1969 to mid-1974. But the problems of devising and managing a complex White House staff remain with the President. The first White House staff organization chart issued in late 1974 had seventy-one boxes in addition to that for the occupant of the Oval Office. (Bonafede 1974: 1956) Moreover, the students of the White House equivalent of Kremlinology were also provided with a floor plan of the West Wing of the White House, so they could, if they wished, measure precedence by charting the number of footsteps that separated select Presidential assistants from his presence.

The experience of the seven Presidents of the United States since Franklin D. Roosevelt shows that Presidential intentions are much more flexible than Presidential institutions. Upon entering office, each President has personal inclinations and political commitments that provide a rough agenda of goals and objectives. Lyndon Johnson and Richard Nixon, each in very different ways, encouraged administrative action, one through legislation and the other by a White House assault upon bureaucratic institutions and processes. John F. Kennedy, otherwise so different from Dwight D. Eisenhower in style and temperament, showed limited interest in major domestic programs.

A President learns on the job what the institutions of the Executive Office of the President can and cannot do for him. Every President is alike in his expectation of Presidential staff: he wants help. Yet the help that White House staff can give him in his personal political capacity is greatly dependent upon his own actions. The help that career officials in such Executive Office agencies as OMB can provide is limited by laws and conventions and by political realities.

From the days of the Brownlow Committee, Presidents have sought to reform the executive branch. The chief area of growth has been in the provision of staff for the President himself. The Brownlow Committee was successful in arguing that the President needs help. In the 1960s Lyndon Johnson and Richard Nixon were successful in seeing that the President's helpers secured help too. But the negative Congressional reaction to the most far-reaching recommendations of the Hoover and the Ash Reports illustrate that there are few things that a President can do to influence the way in which the great institutions of the executive branch are themselves organized.

The President cannot spend much time worrying about how to get the organization right. He has more immediately important tasks to undertake to secure his own re-election and to maintain a political status that rarely depends upon a reputation for attention to management detail. (Herbert Hoover was probably the last President who saw himself as expert in management.) Even if the President believed that he had found the right way to organize the federal executive, there is a high probability that Congress would not allow him to put his ideas into effect. Yet a President cannot be indifferent to how the federal executive organizes its activities, for the program choices that are put to him, and the snarls and disputes that are also put to him both reflect the capability of officials who are meant to serve the President, albeit at some removes from him. Anything the President can do to improve the management of government is potentially beneficial to him in his task of giving direction to his Administration.

The most and the least a President can do in management terms is to sponsor one or two changes which would benefit himself and, incidentally, also leave the office strengthened for his successors. William Howard Taft, by launching a report on governmental economy, stimulated the creation of a Bureau of the Budget a decade after he left office. Franklin D. Roosevelt strengthened the President's personal influence by securing Congressional approval for a small White House staff with a passion for anonymity and a talent for relating their boss's wishes to the political realities of Washington politics. Lyndon Johnson thought he saw in PPBS a means by which the President of the United States could make decisions as readily and profitably as could the President of a successful business firm; he was disappointed in his hope. Richard Nixon left behind him in the White House a Domestic Council, the institutional embodiment of a policy planning staff for which many of his predecessors had yearned.

In addition, Nixon left behind in the Office of Management and Budget a new management-by-objectives system intended to tie in the President's objectives with the actions of career officials with hands-on control of the operating agencies of government. Because this innovation is concerned with both political objectives and the management of ongoing activities within the executive branch, analyzing it in depth is an excellent way to advance understanding of the problems of governing raised in these first three chapters.

# 4

# Introducing
# a New Technique

*These objectives will not simply be identified and then filed away and forgotten. Specific results are to be achieved by specific deadlines. These commitments will be reviewed continually and will guide day to day operations until the objectives are met.*

Richard M. Nixon, *Budget Message of the President*, January, 1974

*He'll (Eisenhower) sit here and he'll say, "Do this! Do that!" And nothing will happen. Poor Ike—it won't be a bit like the Army. He'll find it very frustrating.*

Harry S. Truman, 1953

Management by objectives was the final effort of the Nixon Administration to strengthen the President's direction of the federal executive. This new technique was intended to give the Executive Office of the President more information about the activities of departments and program managers "out there." The information could then be used to stimulate top down directives from Presidential appointees to ensure that career officials were responsive and effective in carrying out the Administration's work. It was also meant to improve the effectiveness of government by concentrating attention upon results. In turn this could give lower-level managers greater discretion in adapting their activities to achieve these results. The Nixon innovators did not see this new technique as a mere management tool, but rather as a way of coming to grips with central problems of political direction and government performance.

In the jargon of management scientists, management by objectives is defined as: "a process whereby the superior and subordinate managers of an organization jointly identify its common goals, define each individual's major areas of responsibility in terms of the results expected of him, and use these measures as guides for operating the unit and assessing the contribution of each of its members." (Odiorne, 1965: 55f) The definition emphasizes three central questions:

1.  What do we want done? (Defining goals in terms of results)
2.  What is each individual expected to contribute to results? (Fixing responsibility)
3.  How are we getting on? (Results used as targets by program managers, and for evaluation by their overseers)

Management by objectives describes a system because of its emphasis upon the relationship between results, responsibilities, and program monitoring. It monitors whether people responsible for activities are progressing toward results agreed upon as desirable.

Management by objectives is neither scientific nor unscientific. The flow charts and diagrams that are its paraphernalia (the system induces visual more than verbal jargon) does not mean that its concepts are abstruse, nor do its methods require specialized training. Management by objectives is a simple business school technique that can be understood and acted upon by men with heavy management responsibilities and no time for social science in the abstract. After having the basic elements of the system explained to him, Frank Clements, Deputy Director of Defense, translated the basic idea thus: "Oh, you mean it's a 'do' list." But management by objectives is more than a list of things to be done. It incorporates procedures for progress chasing as well, to make sure that people do what they are supposed to do. Roy Ash (1973: 2), director of OMB at the time the system was introduced, went to some length to emphasize that the system could as easily be labelled "Management by Common Sense." But he went on to note that commonsense procedures may be prized commodities because in short supply.

In analytic terms, management by objectives is best understood as a very simple cybernetic model of governing. (Rose, 1973: 468) Political leaders are expected to know the direction in which they wish government to go, and they (or their subordinates) are expected to make progress toward these objectives. Failure to make progress is not interpreted as a defeat, but rather as a warning to think again, and select different program means, or even change objectives. The model thus assumes no more than would be assumed by passengers (or crewmen) on a ship. The captain is supposed to know in what direction he wishes the ship to go, and how to steer it there. When storms arise, keeping afloat may be the prime concern of the steersman. But if the captain has no idea where he wishes to head when storms cease, then he is not steering the ship, but simply adrift.

In political terms, management by objectives (MbO) is a control system. But it does not assume a unilateral exercise of power from a central command position, as in the monocratic model of the Presidency. Instead, it assumes, consistent with constitutional practice, that the White House should be regularly informed about the most significant actions of executive departments, and that the President should be able to issue directives in response to such information. It could be argued that the directives would as often be controlled by the knowledge fed into the White House as events are controlled by Presidential directives. In a system with continuing feedback, whether concerned with central heating or with government, the overall goal is the adaptation of actions in a changing environment. Questions of power tend to get lost in the analysis of interactions. For example, one does not ask whether the most powerful factor in central heating is the man who sets the regulator, the thermostat, or the forces that determine the outdoor temperature. Each is important; together they determine a room's temperature.

The introduction of management by objectives was intended to strengthen the Presidency's oversight of the executive branch. Since the inauguration of John F. Kennedy, White House staff had intermittently and often unpredictably sought to find out what was going on out there in the agencies. The motive for such forays was often the suspicion that whatever was happening was inconsistent with the President's wishes. But suspicious inquiries invite guarded responses. Friction was a major product of the flow of communication. By establishing a regular agenda of items subject to White House supervision and regular reporting dates, the sponsors of management by objectives hoped to increase the flow of information to the Executive Office about important programs, while simultaneously reducing resistance by operating agencies. Of itself, improved oversight does not increase the President's influence upon activities of the executive branch. But it does give the Executive Office information that can be used as the basis for going deeper into operating activities, if this is believed to be in the interests of the Presidency.

Textbook definitions of management by objectives emphasize that objectives are not to be imposed unilaterally from the top down; Odiorne recommends that superiors and subordinates should "jointly identify its common goals." Such an assumption is consistent with political practice in the executive branch. While the President is the Chief Executive, responsibility for action is in the hands of career officials whose work is circumscribed by Acts of Congress. The achievement of objectives requires cooperation between Presidential staff, enunciating objectives that they regard as most important from their perspective, and bureau chiefs and career officials who must do what Congress and clients, as well as the President, expect of them. In this way, the President's concern with choice and the career official's concern with what gets done are brought together in a single monitoring process.

Management by objectives is consistent with the emphasis upon program results that has been prominent in Washington since the mid-1960s. Government programs are expected to produce results registered in the lives of American citizens, and not simply to produce results that are registered by the enumeration of money spent, personnel employed, and official files generated. Information about the results of federal programs is not routinely brought before Presidential appointees. Maurice Stans summed up the conventional situation when he asked, in the midst of reviewing expenditure proposals placed before him as Secretary of Commerce, "How come I never get any reports about what happens with this money?"

The origin of management by objectives in business school teaching gives the approach a paternity congenial to Republicans, since such schools are regarded as far less likely to be infected by liberal or spendthrift ideas than are university departments of economics. Yet the more important fact is that business schools (like businessmen) are concerned with problems of management. The Nixon Administration found management consultants and staff with MBAs (Master of Business Administration) congenial, because such men were trained to think in terms of directing large organizations by influencing their continuing activities. Insofar as this emphasis upon management was justified in terms of making established programs operate more efficiently and effectively, liberals could not quarrel, for liberal proponents of programs to improve society suffer politically if government is thought to be inefficient or ineffectual in managing what it attempts.

Although MbO was introduced to government by two graduates of the Harvard Business School, Roy Ash and Frederic V. Malek, they did not see their task in terms of a simple transference to government of what might be effective in private industry. Differences between government and private management were recognized by them and their staff. The most obvious difference is that money measures of performance are not central in government, as they are in private enterprise. The experience of trying to do cost-benefit analysis of the federal government's nonmarket goods has made this clear. At no time was management by objectives promoted as a money-saving device, the public sector equivalent of money making in private industry. A second difference is that the objectives of a business show greater stability; the aim of profit is constantly present, whereas in government the program objectives of Presidential appointees are much more sensitive to short-term alterations as events and political conditions change. A third difference is that Presidential appointees, the men expected to identify objectives and manage to achieve them, are likely to come in from outside the department and depart again in less than two years. In private industry, by contrast, personnel turnover is expected to be lower; individuals who set objectives are still there when the results are at hand. A fourth difference is that lines of responsibility can be much more clearly defined in private corporations, and individuals made responsible, than is possible in government. In the words of former HEW Secretary John W. Gardner, "When you figure out how to hold a middle-level bureaucrat accountable, it'll be comparable to landing on the moon." (Quoted in Brady, 1973: 66) The separation of powers between the executive branch and Congress, and the division of powers through federalism, make apportionment of credit difficult when things go well, and make the avoidance of responsibility easy when things do not go according to plan. Fifthly, public officials are paid a flat salary rather than being paid by results, like a salesman in private industry, or enjoying bonuses or stock options, rewards used to motivate managers who succeed in meeting management objectives.

The harshest critics of management by objectives would argue that the obstacles to MbO in government can also be found in private industry. From this they would conclude that if the system worked in government as it did in private industry it would only generate a large amount of paper and a disproportionate amount of anxieties and pathological behavior within the organizations involved. (See Levinson, 1970; cf. McConkey, 1972)

Management by objectives differs from budgeting, in that it is concerned with the consequences of government actions, and not their costs. The assumption that the budget is "a series of goals with price tags attached" (Wildavsky, 1974: 2) will not stand up to careful scrutiny. The line-item descriptions and program headings of the budget cannot easily be translated into statements of objectives or goals, as the experience of PPBS has demonstrated. The budget shows how much money is being spent by the federal government, which agencies and laws control spending, and what officials may do with the money. It does not show what the government gets for its money, or what it wishes to purchase. The functional categories of the budget are far too broad to provide specific guidance for monitoring the activities of government agencies. The MbO system was intended to concentrate upon action.

The MbO system can concentrate attention upon "priceless" concerns of government, as well as upon action measured in public expenditure statements. Some objectives, such as reducing Aid to Families with Dependent Children benefits paid ineligible recipients, cost little in cash terms, and may even show a profit to government. They can nonetheless be politically significant. The MbO system is like a budget review in that it is not so much concerned with the baseline activities of government, but rather, with what is changing.

The MbO system can consider what is different in a department's proposals for the coming year, whether expressed in terms of money inputs, or the results that are expected to follow from spending or other increments. The MbO system differs from budgeting, in that it asks a department to indicate the most important changes it wishes to achieve in literary form. By contrast, budget examiners infer objectives by investigating claims for new objects of expenditure, or major dollar increases in annual requests.

By contrast with PPBS, management by objectives is intended to decrease paperwork reporting by subordinates. Presidential appointees do not wish to make decisions for bureau chiefs or program managers. Their chief concern is that the activities of subordinates are consistent with their own objectives. (See Niskanen, 1971) The motivational assumption of MbO is succinctly stated by Frederic V. Malek (1974: 6): "Never tell people how to do things. Tell them what to do and they will surprise you with their ingenuity." The point of the MbO mechanism is not to influence decisions in the abstract, but rather to influence events, by making sure that intentions stated are in fact carried out with the promptness that their relative importance deserves. From this perspective, the system is not intended to affect the direction of government, but to improve the speed and certainty with which government agencies carry out commitments to move in agreed ways.

The basic problem in introducing any new techniques is to translate disembodied concepts into specific and immediate tasks of men in charge of organizations with the capability to realize them. The PPBS experiment demonstrated that analytic statements, however well defined on paper, are not effective by themselves because decisions are taken by institutions—e.g., the Bureau of Reclamation, the Bureau of the Budget, or Congressional committees—and not by analysts who freely link concepts in the abstract. Objectives that cannot be related to specific departments of the federal government and, even more, to particular bureaus or accountable officials, are empty rhetorical statements, just as organizational activities without objectives are literally purposeless. The ideal was described by a McKinsey and Company (1970: 7) study prepared for the Bureau of the Budget in the days of PPBS. Anticipating the MbO focus upon accountable organizational units, it declared that political oversight of departments "should ultimately lead to a 'contract' between the agency head and his building block manager to produce specified results for specified resource inputs."

The Department of Health, Education and Welfare was the organizational proving ground for the introduction of management by objectives to the federal executive in the Nixon Administration. A torrent of Great Society legislation had flooded HEW with new programs whose promises were greater than the Department could immediately fulfil. Any newly appointed Secretary faced extreme difficulties of managing or giving direction to his Department. As its name makes evident, HEW is a conglomerate holding company for a variety of health, education and welfare programs with distinctive clienteles and interest groups. Many of the constituent agencies within HEW antedate the creation of the Department in 1953. Many bureaus are concerned with programs that are administered by state and local government. Upwards of 90 per cent of the HEW budget is money sent elsewhere to be spent either by social security benefici- aries or the 40,000 state and local government or nonprofit institu- tions in receipt of HEW grants. A significant portion of departmental staff works from ten regional headquarters spread from Boston to Seattle. Each of these operating bureaus is subject to continuous Congressional oversight, independent of such oversight as might come from the President, or from a Secretary whose term of office is likely to be far briefer than the tenure of agency heads within the department.

The problem of an incoming Secretary of Health, Education and Welfare is analogous to that of an incoming President: learning about the ongoing programs and objectives driven by the forces of political inertia, and deciding what influence he could and should have upon the direction of departmental work. In 1969 Republicans were particularly anxious to get a handle on HEW, because of the size of its budget appropriations, doubts about the efficiency and effective- ness of its activities, and a political belief that the agency had gone too far in welfare commitments that could not or should not be the responsibility of the federal government. The new Secretary, Robert Finch, invited Frederic V. Malek, a former McKinsey and Company management consultant, to become Deputy Under-Secretary and "do something" about the sprawling organization of the government's biggest-spending department. Malek assembled a small staff, and set about investigating what the problems were. A management report of January, 1970 enumerated four main management functions and concluded:

*We are not performing any of these functions in DHEW.*

1. Agencies and regions have only a vague concept of Secretary's priorities.
2. We make no requests and issue no directives to agencies or regions.
3. We receive no information to evaluate performance other than sporadic requests for approval.
4. We do not check on agency or regional progress toward predeter- mined goals in a comprehensive or consistent manner.

The diagnosis was not concerned with technical questions; instead, the management group confronted questions of power. If the Secretary does not have any objectives or fails to communicate them to operating units within the Department, he cannot provide political direction. If the operating staff of HEW have any sense of direction, it comes from some place else than the nominal head of the department, the Office of the Secretary.

Management by objectives was prescribed as one mechanism useful to remedy faults at HEW. (For details see Malek, 1971; Brady, 1973; Marik and McFee, 1974) The first manual described the Operational Planning System, as the MbO process became known in the department, as helping "fill the gap between the long-range planning and budgeting process, and ultimate evaluation of program effectiveness." The system is thus outside the scope of the "politics of choice" and the "politics of evaluation," major staff activities administered through the Assistant Secretary for Planning and Evaluation. It focusses instead upon whether the department has managed to follow through with action, once choices are made. It is administered from the office of the Deputy Assistant Secretary for Management Planning and Technology, under the Assistant Secretary for Administration and Management.

As institutionalized in HEW under Elliott Richardson as Secretary, the MbO system involved a complex six-step series of exchanges between the Office of the Secretary and agency heads responsible for operating programs. (Brady 1973: 68f) The Secretary's initiatives tend to be confined to giving general guidance to agency heads about problems that he considers important in the coming fiscal year. Specific objectives are then formulated by lower-echelon officials. These are sent up to the Secretary for discussion, and approval or modification. From the lengthy list of things that agency heads wish to do, the Secretary can then select upwards of seventy objectives (that is, about ten per operating division) to monitor from his office. Agency heads, bureau chiefs under them, and regional directors altogether have identified up to 1,800 objectives in a year. The Secretary's influence is confined to the identification of areas of high problem visibility, the refinement or reshaping of agency objectives submitted in draft form, and the selection of objectives for high-level monitoring. The identification and precise formulation of objectives is in the hands of operating units within the department. It is hoped that program managers will regard objectives as meaningful and be committed to their achievement.

A small staff in the office of the Assistant Secretary for Administration and Management at HEW monitors progress on a monthly basis, and prepares progress reports for bimonthly conferences between the Secretary and responsible program officials. The conferences permit two-way communication between the Secretary and program managers; the latter can report progress and difficulties to the Secretary, and he can give his emphasis and direction about priorities and disputes. The conduct of these small conferences is partly dependent upon the personality of the Secretary. Elliott Richardson's use of the conferences as a principal mechanism of dialogue with subordinates gave them their greatest significance. The amount of dialogue lessened with Secretary Caspar Weinburger.

The continuance of the MbO system under three temperamentally different Secretaries is an indicator that the system has some usefulness to those who are responsible for giving direction to the department. The process is not without its critics within the department. (See, e.g., Harvard Business School, 1972) The most frequent complaints are the amount of paperwork generated ("We have a tendency to play office the way kids play house") and the limited commitment of lower-echelon staff to identifying priorities through MbO. In Malek's judgment:

> This is clearly far from a perfect system. It has, however, significantly improved ability to objectively measure performance. We are no longer required to rely on proxy measures such as long hours, lunch at the desk, and large backlogs. The system has also been useful in keeping attention focussed on issues and problems that are no longer on the center stage but still need concentrated follow through for their successful implentation. (Malek, 1971: 15)

A long-service HEW official evaluated its achievement more succinctly: "To see how much we have improved you have to look back at how bad things used to be here."

The introduction of management by objectives to the federal executive as a whole followed the appointment of Roy Ash (formerly head of Litton Industries) as director of OMB, and Frederic Malek as deputy director, in early 1973. Principal responsibility for institutionalizing MbO was taken by Malek, a self-styled professional manager, who was prevailed upon to stay in government by the opportunity to reform the way in which it went about its business. In addition to business success and experience of HEW, Malek brought to his new job important political credentials. After eighteen months at HEW, he had gone to the White House to take charge of personnel work, recruiting and evaluating candidates for Presidential appointments. After the Watergate incident, he was assigned to help straighten out the running of the Nixon campaign by CREP, returning to the White House to assist Roy Ash in the reassignment of personnel and reorganization of Presidential lines of communication with the agencies following Nixon's landslide victory in November, 1972. The new deputy director had no special experience of budgeting. While Malek developed an interest in the subject, and attended many budget meetings during the Autumn budget review, he regarded it as of only short-term significance. The improvement of management—through MbO and through better recruitment and training of public officials—was his chief concern.

The Office of Management and Budget was the obvious choice as lead agency to introduce a new management system throughout the federal executive. Since 1939, along with budgeting, management has been one of its two major responsibilities. Moreover, officials of the Bureau were aware that in government management is part of a *political* process. The complaints by Harold Smith (1945: 33ff) about "the subtle resistances that mass organizations set up against the initiative of management . . . [that is], bureaucratic sabotage" and of the tendency of management "to lose sight of the main objectives by overconcentration on procedures and forms" echoed meaningfully in Washington after the Great Society programs had reached their legislative apogee and crashed in a no-man's-land of administrative obstacles. The management side of OMB, moreover, was in need of new impetus. In the words of a 1967 Bureau of the Budget self-evaluation, management was "a depressed area . . . which has been looking too long at the same problems and has gone stale." In 1970 a public administration scholar concluded, "The history of management improvement in the federal government is a story of inflated rhetoric, shifting emphasis from one fashionable managerial skill to another, and a relatively low level of professional achievement." (Bernstein, 1970: 515f)

The creation of the newly styled Office of Management and Budget did not of itself make management pre-eminent within that agency, although it was, with 146 professional staff, second only to budgeting, with 233 professionals, in the size of its staff. In 1971 a Performance Measurement System was launched; it was a hangover from PPBS in the elaborateness of its framework and demands made for information. It did not survive the pilot stage. By October, 1971 a conference of federal managers concluded with two-thirds suggesting "OMB should let the agencies manage" and avoid "the latest fads and gimmickry." (Mullaney, 1971: 2387) Frank Carlucci, then Associate Director for Management, was cautiously determined: "The overall goal of managing government is to improve the quality of service delivered to people. It is one thing to make a pronouncement. It's another to make sure that that's what happens at the ultimate level—down where the rubber hits the ground, so to speak. To do this effectively, you need to set goals and have timetables." Murray Comarow, executive director of the Ash Council, which recommended the creation of OMB, was cautiously sceptical in viewing its management achievements: "They haven't done any miracles. On the other hand, institutions are very hard to turn around. It's just damn hard to make people change." (Mullaney 1971: 2378)

To the management side of OMB, Fred Malek brought the political standing acquired by working in an important and sensitive White House position, the support of the Director of OMB for his efforts to do something to improve management throughout the federal executive, and a new technique that promised to engage Presidential attention. Immediately upon appointment, Malek established a small staff in the Old Executive Office Building to work day and night preparing for the introduction of management by objectives throughout the executive branch.

To make sure that management by objectives had a priority claim for attention within OMB, Malek secured the creation of a new category of staff—management associates—to be solely responsible for the MbO system. In an agency that is perennially short of staff, thirty posts were allocated to it, a substantial commitment compared to the assignment of twelve men to deal with the whole of Evaluation and Program Implementation. The management associates were divided into four broad program groups parallel to but separate from budget examiners. Each group reports to a Deputy Associate Director for Management. Malek himself had only one senior professional assistant, Robert Wallace, plus personal assistants. The management associates, like budget examiners, have come from a wide variety of backgrounds. The majority have had previous government experience, usually with an operating department rather than within OMB itself.

The bulk of MbO staff is in the twenty-one major departments and agencies operating the system. Responsibility is fixed with an Assistant Secretary for Administration and Management, the Under-Secretary, or his functional equivalent, depending upon the structure of a department. MbO personnel are thus placed in between the top staff working in the Office of the Secretary, and line managers with hands-on control of programs. Because they report to an official with broad management functions cutting across the organizational units of a department, MbO staff have access to a routine flow of paper concerning departmental activities. To ensure that the right sort of people are responsible for MbO in the departments, Malek vetted the qualifications of many assigned responsibility there. He had already supervised the appointment of a number of persons, including ex-White House staff, to Under-Secretary and Assistant Secretary positions while at the White House the previous autumn. Day-to-day responsibility for running MbO activities within a department was normally assigned to career officials already experienced in administration and management within the department.

In the distribution of staff, MbO resembled PPBS, for the introduction of PPBS in 1965 had added 350 professionals to attend to its work in twenty-one agencies, as against the addition of about twenty professionals in the Bureau of the Budget. (See Ott and Ott, 1969: 48) Management by objectives did not, however, create large specialist staff in the departments. Instead, except for a few relatively junior officials concerned with routine paper-pushing tasks, management by objectives is supposed to be one among several concerns of supervisory staff with a variety of powers that they could use to push programs forward. The low profile approach in promoting MbO reflected a conscious awareness that several years after the unlamented death of PPBS, acronymic techniques were still anathema to most department officials.

After two months preparation, management by objectives was launched in the executive branch with the full authority of the President. On April 18, 1973, a letter from Richard Nixon went to each department or major agency head asking for "an outline of major goals and objectives for your organization to be accomplished during the coming year" in order to gain "a sharper focus on the results which the various activities under your direction are aimed at achieving." Concurrently, a memorandum was sent by Roy Ash, Director of OMB, making explicit what each head of department was expected to do to meet the President's request, and the deadline date when statements of objectives would soon be due.

Ironically, no single, precise, measurable statement of the objectives of the management-by-objectives system was issued by the Office of Management and Budget. (Cf. Chapter 9) Both Ash and Malek stressed that the new system was not a mechanical device to assure dollars-and-cents savings, or decide between competing programs, but rather a pervasive and general attitude of mind. In Ash's view, "It's a way of doing what comes naturally. It isn't a new process, it isn't a bunch of reports, it isn't a set series of meetings. . . . It's a new style, not a new process." Ash was enthusiastic enough to suggest that MbO could "make program analysis a year-round activity, with budget decisions flowing from it." (Havemann, 1973: 783) Malek emphasized the long-term advantages that might be gained from changing the outlook of career officials whose activities contribute so much to the inertia movement of government:

*We desperately needed MbO on a government-wide basis. Too many people thought that management referred only to administrative and housekeeping activities. We had to change the way they thought about their jobs. They were running around, jumping from hot spot to hot spot.*

*I think 10 years from now we're not going to be remembered for specific results on any given objective, but for institutionalizing a new way of managing the government and changing the way people think about their jobs.*

# 5

# Identifying Objectives

*All too often uncertainty about objectives leads to a trap that might be called "management by activity." This is a euphoric state of mind which equates more with better, which suggests that, as doing good things produces good results, doing twice as many good things will quite obviously produce twice as many good results. In other words, if you don't know where you're going, run faster.*

Elliott Richardson, 1972

While philosophers and social scientists can debate endlessly whether or not government has objectives, public officials in downtown Washington cannot allow themselves time for doubt. Management associates were appointed to make the MbO system work. The system required the identification of objectives, and the President explicitly asked departments for such statements. Management associates therefore expected to get answers, not philosophical evasions, in their dialogues with departments.

Management associates approached their work by assuming that the objectives of government (like total public expenditure) would be the sum of the objectives of individual agencies. It was assumed that if the twenty-one agencies accounting for nearly 95 per cent of federal expenditure were asked to state their objectives for the coming fiscal year, they would have something to say in reply. By concentrating attention upon objectives capable of achievement within the forthcoming year, OMB officials hoped to avoid wrangles about ultimate objectives or about the inadequacies of long-term planning. Emphasis was placed upon the immediate consequences of actions taken by departments making continuing demands upon the Executive Office for money, legislation, and political support.

By directing requests for objectives to the head of major government departments, OMB officials ensured, from the beginning that objectives could be related to organizational units responsible for them. This avoided the problem that often plagues functional analysis or analysis of government in terms of clients or some other nonorganizational unit—the inability to identify any particular agency or bureau as specifically responsible for a function. Within a given department, the Secretary was expected to provide some sense of selectivity and coordination in filtering statements submitted to him by bureau chiefs, the units typically responsible for preparing a given objective. Reliance upon the departments also meant that the MbO staff did not commit themselves to rank objectives between departments, or eliminate inconsistencies or bridge gaps revealed when objectives were viewed centrally. The program is not intended to coordinate activities that are not otherwise coordinated within the executive branch.

The first priority of management associates was to keep departments to a demanding timetable for processing statements of objectives. Until OMB could demonstrate that it was possible to institutionalize management by objectives within the federal executive, the value of MbO would only be hypothetical. [Cf. Wildavsky's explanation for the failure of PPBS: "No one knows how to do program budgeting." (1974: 201)] To maintain the momentum of the President's initial letter (and in recognition of the fact, both quoted and exemplified by Malek, that Presidential appointees average less than two years in a job), OMB established an action-forcing series of immediate deadlines. Individual agencies were expected to submit their initial year's statement of objectives for the next fiscal year within two to eight weeks of the President's initial letter of April 18, 1973. As the fiscal year started on July 1, OMB was under great pressure to review statements internally, send them to the Domestic Council for comment, discuss them with agency heads, and refer them to the President before the fiscal year was too far advanced. The objectives were sent to the White House for Presidential approval at the end of the summer, and the President issued individual letters to department heads, endorsing their statements without amendment on September 25. OMB and departmental staff then commenced monitoring progress toward Presidentially approved objectives three months after the fiscal year had begun.

Before OMB and departmental staff had had a full year's experience in monitoring and registering the achievement of objectives, the imperatives of the calendar required the beginning of another annual catalog of objectives. On March 22, 1974, the President issued a call to agencies "to press toward meeting the goals for fiscal year 1974 and to determine a new set of objectives for fiscal year 1975." The second year's cycle, building upon experience, was completed in six months. On September 12, 1974, President Ford issued letters to each participating agency head endorsing their statements of Presidential objectives without amendment. By midsummer, 1975, federal officials had thus accumulated two year's experience in running a management-by-objectives system; this provides the materials analyzed here. It is ample to reveal MbO's strengths and weaknesses.

The initial OMB directive was noteworthy for its nondirectiveness. Departments were asked to submit objectives, subject only to the following criteria:

1. The issue or initiative is important to the President.
2. There is a method to determine if the item has been accomplished.
3. It can be generally met within existing or currently planned resources.

The third qualification was inserted to emphasize the difference between the budget process, concerned with how much money departments received, and the MbO system, concerned with what managers use money for. By directing attention away from budgetary and legislative concerns (where President Nixon was not an expansionist like his predecessor), OMB hoped to turn the attention of departments from the more glamorous areas of government growth to the Administration's own chief priority: the more effective and efficient operation of established programs, and the implementation of new Administration commitments. In addition, the MbO system was meant to make departments think harder at the precommittal stage of program development, that is, to make explicit the objectives that new budget commitments and new legislation should achieve, and not to assume that "more means better."

In approaching departments, OMB leaned over backward in an attempt to emphasize that they were not being asked to transcribe in their own handwriting lists that had been prepared from above, or to adopt prescribed procedures to meet central procedures. OMB's initial circular to departments stated: "OMB does not intend to present a manual to the Department on how the effort is to operate. We urge the Department to think carefully about what are its own unique characteristics, what comparable efforts are underway in the Department and what will work for them." In Fred Malek's words (1974: 6), "The emphasis is on a person-to-person dialogue with a minimum amount of paperwork. No written reports are required from the agencies, and personal contact is the primary means of communication at all organizational levels." The invitation to think about the objectives of actions, rather than procedure, unnerved some bureaucrats who found safety and contentment in concentrating upon procedures for their own sake. One HUD official complained to a journalist, "OMB is being so flexible I can't stand it." (Havemann, 1974: 611)

The President's letter launching the management-by-objectives system was treated by OMB as a stimulus to departments. It was not intended as a White House effort to mandate priorities upon departments; such an effort would have been ineffectual in the aftermath of Watergate in any event. It was feared that objectives imposed from above by an OMB management group with little more than one man per department would "hit the department and run off, like water off a duck's back." To emphasize the importance of departmental involvement, Ash and Malek made a point of going to department headquarters for their initial meetings about MbO, rather than calling agency heads into the Old Executive Office Building. In the words of one OMB official, the system started "a dialogue in which we ask the questions and they provide the answers." The guidance given each department was a memorandum prepared by management associates listing "areas to be considered in the development of department objectives." The annexes were compilations of budget submission statements, Presidential messages, and other pre-existing policy statements. In the words of one agency official, "Our MbO list could have come from reading the newspapers."

The short time allowed for the preparation of the initial year's statement of objectives, as well as the intrinsic organizational difficulty of doing anything for the first time, meant that OMB management associates were in a weak position vis-a-vis departments in their initial meetings. Management associates were anxious that the department assigned to them report *some* objectives. Agencies varied enormously in terms of the cooperativeness and competence of their response. Without explicit central directives and without the experience of operating the system for the previous year, agencies were more or less left to define objectives as they wished. Unlike budget examiners, who make recommendations about departmental finances, management associates had no sanction that they could bring against a department. The exclusion of a departmental proposal from a list would deny an activity the status of Presidential recognition—but it would not stop a department from making it a departmental objective. A department that failed to turn in any objectives in the first year could operate on a business as usual basis from the force of inertia.

OMB successfully met its first priority: twenty of twenty-one agencies receiving the President's request to submit objectives did in fact make returns in the first summer of the program's operation. The twenty-one agencies involved embraced all Cabinet departments as well as ACTION, the Atomic Energy Commission, CIA, the Civil Service Commission, the Environmental Protection Agency, the General Services Administration, the National Science Foundation, NASA, the Small Business Administration, and the Veterans Administration. This combination of prominent and not so prominent federal agencies together account for nearly 95 per cent of the federal budget. In the second year, the Federal Energy Administration also filed objectives. Initially, only the State Department did not. An unidentified State Department spokesman explained:

> We know what our objectives are in a very broad sense. But it is awfully difficult to measure progress in foreign policy. The only activity the department can measure with any precision is the distribution of passports and visas. . . .
>
> In many cases we do not control our own destiny. We cannot state how we are going to cope except in the most general of terms, and OMB wants precision. (Havemann, 1973: 792; 1974: 612)

In the second year, the State Department too submitted objectives.

The visible outputs of the MbO process are the documents cataloguing objectives approved by the President. In the absence of OMB guidelines or established federal operating procedure, departmental submissions to OMB vary considerably in format, terminology, and analytic sophistication. There are also inconsistencies in practice within a single agency. Hence, the first stage in analysis is to establish standard terminology, as a precondition of judging objectives, quantitatively and qualitatively.

In its initial circular, OMB analysts defined the crucial concept *objectives* in a manner meaningful in the context of the federal government: "The most important accomplishments that the Department can reasonably attain during the next four to 18 months." In ordinary language, it was asking the Department to say: What will be different because of your efforts about a year from now? For each objective listed, the department was also asked to identify *milestones*, that is, actions that the department intends to take by a stated date in the coming months as a means of attaining an objective. When the concerns of a department extend beyond the coming fiscal year (e.g., NASA) it is allowed to identify long-term *goals*, conditions capable of attainment or approach in the more distant future.

In the majority of departmental documents, objectives and milestones are clearly identified. But sometimes a department lists two objectives in a single numbered sentence with a compound predicate. In other instances, a statement entered as an objective, e.g., "to further DoD's social and human goals," is best considered a long-term goal or ideal, and measures described as milestones treated as the department's objectives in the next fiscal year. In a few cases, e.g., the Department of Labor, the first year's objectives were stated in prose paragraphs of such length and complexity that it would be difficult for an outside analyst, or for that matter, departmental staff, to be clear about the specific action implications of a statement.

The tortuous nature of bureaucratic prose is a symptom of thought processes characteristic of public officials who produce intra-agency and interagency memoranda. They do not think of their work as does an operations research scientist, carefully specifying each element in mathematical symbols, then joining the different elements together by a mathematical equation to indicate a result. Nor are statements written with the simple cause-and-effect clarity of instructions for a coin-operated vending machine: "If you want this, do that." The language of Washington bureaucracy is as convoluted yet less precise than the law, and as ephemeral yet less readable than journalism. It is the language of politics.

The weak logical structure of many statements of Presidential objectives is evidenced by the difficulty in counting the total number of objectives endorsed in each of the program's first two years. The tables that follow are based upon statements of objectives from nineteen of twenty departments participating in 1974, omitting only the CIA, and twenty of twenty-two departments participating in 1975, omitting only the CIA and Defense. To identify milestones, objectives, and longer-term goals with consistentcy and consistent with the logic of management by objectives meant renumbering a variety of departmental submissions, in order to put each into a standard logical form. (Cf. Chapter 6) The resulting enumeration produced 237 objectives for 1974 and 225 in 1975.

The subject matter of 1974 Presidential objectives reflects a combination of persisting concerns and the circumstances of the moment. The most frequently cited concern—the improvement of agency management—is relevant to all departments at all times. But the subjects that follow in frequency—the economy, the environment and natural resources, and energy—very much reflect a point in time when America's wealth of resources could no longer to be taken for granted. The frequency with which objectives refer to health, housing, social welfare, and space reflects the continuing importance of such issues in Washington and in the country. The attention given new federalism and minority employment in 1974 and 1975 reflects the particular political judgments and priorities of the President. The only topic substantially under-represented by comparison with its significance in the budget is education, the subject of one objective in each year. In part, this is due to the limited federal responsibility for education. It also reflects the tendency of HEW to concentrate attention upon health and welfare issues. (See Table 5.1)

The change in the occupancy of the White House between the promulgation of the 1974 and 1975 Presidential objectives is not reflected in any change in their subject matter. The biggest change, an increased attention given energy questions, is a reflection of world trends, rather than personal or partisan priorities. The fluctuations in emphasis between the first and second year reflect more or less random variations.

All departments show concern with a variety of subjects, in keeping with the heterogeneous demands made by their clients, by Congress, and by their own bureau chiefs. More than half the objectives of an agency usually fall within a single broad subject area, but the remainder reflect a myriad ramification of concerns. For example, while five of Agriculture's 1974 objectives concerned farming, the remainder were dispersed among economic affairs, social welfare, housing, the environment, minority employment, and management improvement. Similarly, Defense included among its objectives minority employment in defense industries, social welfare (the military's drug abuse program), and energy (reducing total energy use

TABLE 5.1.  The Subject of Presidential Objectives, 1974 and 1975

| | OBJECTIVES 1974* | | OBJECTIVES 1975* | |
|---|---|---|---|---|
| TOPICS | *N* | % | *N* | % |
| Departmental management | 45 | 19 | 44 | 19 |
| The economy | 34 | 14 | 32 | 14 |
| Environment and natural resources | 21 | 9 | 15 | 7 |
| Energy | 15 | 6 | 21 | 9 |
| New federalism | 13 | 5.5 | 10 | 4 |
| Minority employment | 13 | 5.5 | 9 | 4 |
| Health | 13 | 5.5 | 10 | 4 |
| Defense | 12 | 5 | (not available) | |
| Foreign affairs | (none prepared) | | 16 | 7 |
| Social welfare | 10 | 4 | 8 | 4 |
| Housing | 9 | 4 | 13 | 6 |
| Space | 9 | 4 | 8 | 4 |
| Crime and administration of justice | 9 | 4 | 4 | 2 |
| Transportation | 8 | 3 | 9 | 4 |
| Government supplies | 8 | 3 | 6 | 3 |
| Agriculture | 5 | 2 | 4 | 2 |
| Veterans | 5 | 2 | 4 | 2 |
| Voluntary work | 4 | 2 | 4 | 2 |
| Indians | 2 | 1 | 4 | 2 |
| Miscellaneous (Bicentennial, education, unclassifiable) | 2 | 1 | 4 | 2 |
| Totals | 237 | 100 | 225 | 100 |

*Here and elsewhere, the reference is to a fiscal year, running twelve months from July 1.

by DoD). There was little evidence of one department poaching another's primary concern. For example, all the objectives concerning veterans came from the Veterans' Administration, nearly all concerning Housing and Community Development came from HUD, and those concerning government supplies, from the General Services Administration. Where departmental jurisdictions are unclear or overlapping and events make a subject of major political significance, then a multiplicity of agencies each signified their interest. Eight different agencies put forward energy objectives, and six environmental objectives. A few topics, such as minority employment and federalism, by their nature affect many departments.

An indirect measure of the extent to which departments have treated the MbO system as a management game irrelevant to major substantive concerns is the extent to which management improvement objectives are cited. The figures in Table 5.1 indicate an average of about two management objectives for each department, a not unreasonable proportion. There are variations between departments. In addition to the management-oriented Civil Service Commission, four other agencies made management improvement the topic of more than one-third of their first year's Presidential objectives: the Veterans Administration (four out of ten), ACTION (two out of five), the Justice Department (four out of thirteen) and HUD (five of eighteen). In 1975, Justice and the VA, as well as HEW, gave a disproportionate attention to management concerns.

The quantity of objectives is less significant than quality. But the question then arises: What makes a good objective? OMB has not offered departments a list of dos and don'ts in the selection of objectives. Management associates within OMB, like their counterparts in the departments, disagree among themselves about the attributes that distinguish good from bad objectives in the MbO system. One reason for disagreement is that decisions about the selection of objectives involve a series of dilemmas for those making the choice. It is in the nature of a dilemma that there is always something to be said for each alternative.

1. *Quantification or meaningfulness.* Critics are quick to assert that political objectives cannot be quantified without being made trivial, thus constituting a fundamental limitation upon the operation of any "business-style" MbO system. As attempts to develop social indicators of social wellbeing have demonstrated (HEW, 1969), it is often difficult to produce suitable quantitative measures for such seemingly simple objectives as health. One way around this problem is to substitute proximate objectives, such as Congressional enactment of a health bill. It is easy enough to verify whether or not an Act of Congress concerning health has been passed, even though one

cannot show what its consequences will be. Another way to meet the problem has been to quantify objectives, even when the quantitative measure is trivial, e.g., the Small Business Administration objective to "increase by four per cent the proportion of total purchases from small business by agencies at which SBA has procurement center representatives," or create a tyranny of numbers, e.g., the Justice Department target to "increase by seven per cent the number of deportable aliens expelled." Both Ash and Malek sought to allay fears that MbO meant Management by Quantification: "Granted, there is a measurability problem, but a lot can be done with non-quantifiable or subjective evaluation techniques if the problem is approached sensibly." (Malek, 1974: 2)

On the other hand, even the most determined critic of quantification would find it difficult to regard as meaningful, simply because it was nonquantitative, a 1975 State Department objective to base foreign policy on "a partnership between the government and people" requiring "a new consensus" concerning "our fundamental interests and evolving aims . . . a realistic view of our capabilities . . . and a positive and open public dialogue on issues."

Numbers can be invoked in contexts where they hide the obscurity of underlying verbal concepts. For example in 1974 HEW had the objective of "reducing unnecessary utilization of medical care under its Medicare and Medicaid programs to achieve savings of $100 mil. and $200 mil. respectively." The appearance of such savings on the books would not be proof that *unnecessary* utilization had been reduced; it could easily be argued that this only meant that costs had been reduced. Purely verbal objectives can also be vague or trivial, as two HUD objectives illustrate. In the first, the key term—to carry out our mission at minimum cost—implies numerical measurement, but the basis of assessment is left unstated. The phrase invites endless dispute about what cost is actually the minimum. In another instance, none of the crucial terms can be related to specific activities: "To evaluate the existing HUD field structure and develop alternatives suitable to executing the changing responsibilities of the department."

2. *Immediate achievements or long-term results.* Managers have a commonsense desire to put first things first. The OMB request for objectives to be realized within the coming fiscal year is consistent with that. But many things important in government, whether the development of energy resources or the simple passage and implementation of an Act of Congress, cannot be achieved within a limited number of months. Departments working in an engineering environment, such as NASA or parts of Interior, have found it relatively straightforward to link fiscal year objectives to longer-term goals,

e.g., phasing development stages of a manned space flight. But social engineering proceeds far less certainly. One of the biggest causes of uncertainty is the fact that politicians may change their minds about directions once every fiscal year—or more often. In such departments as HEW there is a tendency to concentrate upon objectives that can be realized within the year, such as "issuing regulations" or "develop options for restructuring" a program or "submit to Congress an Administration proposal." Such statements have the advantage of concentrating the attention of managers upon immediate concerns, and producing results promptly for OMB. Yet they also reinforce a tendency that James Clarke, Assistant Secretary for Administration at Interior, has identified as wishing "to think of what they're going to do rather than what is going to be accomplished by what they do." (Havemann, 1974: 1201)

3. *"Bigger" or smaller objectives.* Because bigger objectives tend to be long-term, less easily quantified or verified and often can only be realized with the help of forces outside the control of a department, many management associates believe that there is no point in trying to hold departments accountable for achievements that are "too big." For example, HEW officials have tended to confine their MbO system to well-defined targets within the ability of the department to achieve by its own efforts. In other words, instead of entering such a goal as "Improving the nation's health," HEW will have an objective such as "Change management improvement in the Comprehansive Health Planning Program." To do this, however, is to remove from the MbO system any concern with major long-term goals, or even important short-term concerns where departmental objectives are unclear or uncertain of achievement. Insofar as this occurs, the system fails to offer the Executive Office of the President a means of stretching departments to take on bigger and more difficult objectives.

The problems facing OMB in seeking "bigger" and "better" objectives was demonstrated in April, 1974, when OMB director Roy Ash, in a letter paralleling the MbO procedure, invited every Cabinet Secretary to submit proposals for "key new thrusts for this Administration as we begin our last 1000 days." The memo asked for their "three best ideas . . . which should be new and imaginative proposals, broad in scope and addressed to the most important public needs." (Havemann, 1974: 921) The only constraints were that the proposals should be capable of accomplishment, or at least, major progress within the three-year period ahead and, if legislation would be required, that a draft bill could be introduced to Congress within the year. Whatever the motives for the Presidential request, the result was clear; departments reiterated established objectives, or suggested expanding already established programs. An OMB circular cannot by itself generate fresh major proposals for the President, especially proposals that will also be politically saleable.

4. *Clear commitment or noncommital objectives.* Almost invariably, management staff emphasize that the precise phrasing of an objective is less important than the extent to which the words are a token of a department's determination to get something done. As one agency official put it: "A poorly written objective can be very important, if the words are those of a manager who is effective in getting things done. Equally, a lot of people around here are good cover men. They can put good-looking objectives down on paper, but this is only to make them look effective when they are not." Malek and his staff were anxious to have departments draft objectives in their own words, rather than pull rank from the Executive Office of the President, believing this the best way to obtain commitment to objectives meaningful to the people who would have to do the work to realize them. From a Presidential perspective, however, it is less certain that commitment to objectives is a good thing—at least, for the President. For the man in the Oval Office to endorse objectives sent up to him from the departments is to give them the right to make commitments on his behalf. An initial endorsement can then become the basis for continuing claims from departments for Presidential assistance in their efforts to achieve "his" objective. One senior OMB official responsible for reviewing statements before passage to the White House considered his role that of making objectives bland or vague, if they touched upon subjects that could otherwise involve the President in controversy. For example, no one could quarrel with the President for endorsing a 1975 Agriculture Department objective "Adequate domestic food supplies offered at reasonable consumer price levels." Such a statement does not commit the President to either party in a continual controversy about farm income and food prices. Another way in which the President can avoid becoming committed on controversial matters of substance is if an objective calls for a report upon an issue—but lays down no indication of what the report will contain. In that way, the President can delay deciding, until after a departmental committee has canvassed alternatives and identified likely political supporters and opponents, whether to commit himself to the recommendations resulting from the achievement of a "first-stage" objective.

It is easier to identify characteristics that will eliminate a departmental statement from the list of Presidential objectives than to prescribe how a good statement should be written. First of all, OMB rejects statements if they are inconsistent with the President's program, as enunciated in State of the Union messages and similar authoritative statements. The identification of objectives is not a process of bringing forward issues for decision by the White House. It is, instead, a means of registering what the President is already committed to do, and fixing responsibility for who will do something about these decisions by a given date. Secondly, a department does not bring forward statements if they reflect discredit upon its work. For example, no department volunteered that it would "clean up the mess in such and such an area," or "try to find out why program X doesn't work after all these years." Thirdly a department will not forward objectives in subject areas where there is a major dispute within it about what it should do, or a major dispute between the department and the Executive Office about what overall Administration policy should be. That these controversies generate objectives "too hot to write down" does not mean they are neglected. The opposite is the case. They are treated as matters of high priority, even urgency. For example, in the Department of Agriculture Secretary Earl Butz himself held fortnightly meetings to monitor progress on Secretarial objectives kept confidential within the department, as well as vis-a-vis OMB, because of their controversial nature. Finally, at the other extreme, OMB will veto statements of departmental objectives on the ground that they lack sufficient political substance to merit White House status. It is not always easy to see the basis for distinguishing between a Presidential level objective (e.g., the 1975 Interior statement: "Implement the Bicentennial program on schedule") and a departmental objective (e.g., the 1975 Interior statement: "Reduce the FY 75 fatal and disabling injury rates in metal and non-metal mines to below those of FY 74"). In departments where the Secretary or his staff strongly support the MbO system, objectives thus downgraded are maintained among a much greater and more detailed list of departmental objectives.

In addition to assessing the quality of objectives, management associates are continually assessing departments and the bureaus within them. They are the operating agencies determining what government does. Management associates can make comparative judgments, because each division monitors a number of departments and agencies. Overall, their experience has led them to believe that there are a lot of agencies that should be better managed. In the extreme case of ACTION, a newly appointed head agreed; he confessed that the MbO project made him realize, "When I came here, there were no goals." (Havemann, 1973: 792) The view of OMB management associates about departmental management is summed up in a few remarks by an official in the economy and general government division. After commenting favorably that several agencies showed a readiness to take actions to improve management, he remarked of one Cabinet department: "It is an uphill battle to get the department to produce ANY objective. They need their hand held, though some are less dim than others. The best I could do was to set up a study group to study what objectives the department might have."

Judgments about objectives, like the statements themselves, have little meaning in isolation. To understand their significance (or their emptiness) they must be examined in the context of the policy process.

# 6

# Locating Objectives in the Policy Process

*Trying to get anything moving around here is like pushing molasses.*

OMB official

Examining objectives for one fiscal year gives a static picture of government; one of its chief features is that activities persist through time. At the start of an Administration, a President may feel that past commitments embodied in legislation, institutions, and, not least, client expectations are deadweight, restraining his accomplishments. Initially, attention will focus upon what he can make happen in his first year in office, or even in his first 100 days. After months of frustrating attempts to move the bureaucracy, his faith in instant government is likely to wane. The longer a President stays in office, the more likely he is to appreciate that the long lead time and inertia of government can be turned to his advantage. If he can once get a program started, the chance that his successor can alter or abandon it is limited. As well as making an impact in the morning headlines, a President may also try to leave monuments in the laws and statutes of the United States and in new program headings in the federal budget.

From the viewpoint of a politician under pressure, the best model to describe the policy process may be one with a time horizon as short as a few months or a few days. When crises are frequent and immediate, the next fiscal year is a long time away. The actions that must be taken are those that get one past the current bottleneck, rather than those affecting anything that may happen after that.

When a policy is in dispute and actions highly uncertain, a politician may prefer to take one step at a time, calculating his next objective only after he sees where his latest achievement has landed him. This style of decision making has been labelled "serial disjointed incrementalism" by Braybrooke and Lindblom (1963), a formal definition of the art of muddling through. The label is particularly appropriate for Congressional politics, where every vote upon a bill can be the last one—if it is negative. The approach of a planner or systems analyst, by contrast, will put last things first, that is, concentrate initially upon long-term goals and, after deciding these, consider what steps are immediately necessary to get there from here.

The management-by-objectives system in theory, at least, integrates both points of view, identifying milestones, fiscal year objectives and long-term goals as elements in the policy process. The multiplicity of stages involved in a single departmental policy can be illustrated by HUD's 1974 proposal: "To develop and implement national housing policies that will foster the opportunity for a decent home and suitable living environment for every American equitably and at a reasonable cost." The statement identifies a long-term goal or ideal that could only be realized many years after an incumbent Secretary or President would be gone from office. It identifies two objectives for the forthcoming fiscal year: preparing recommendations for a major new initiative in federal housing policy, and developing proposals to improve the management and conservation of federally subsidized or insured housing. The milestones for each of these objectives consist of a series of reports, meetings, and committee decisions, all to be completed by target deadlines (e.g., September 7, transmitting a new housing initiative to Congress; September 30, preparing a comprehensive plan for housing maintenance). The achievement of the two 1974 objectives would not mean that HUD had reached its long-term housing goal. But it cannot hope to move toward it until after the preconditions identified as milestones and objectives for fiscal year 1974 are achieved.

Government policies are the product of a complex series of actions; they are thus best described as part of a policy *process*, rather than as the result of policy making, which implies choices realized at a single point in time. The architects of the MbO system appreciated this, and the reporting requirements placed upon agencies reflect a readiness to follow through several stages of activities.

The basic sequence of events and influences is outlined in the flow chart in Figure 6.1. Milestones are the immediate concern of government officials. They are specific, recognizable steps that are a precondition of achieving a given objective. For example, if the objective is the issuance of a report on a controversial issue, then

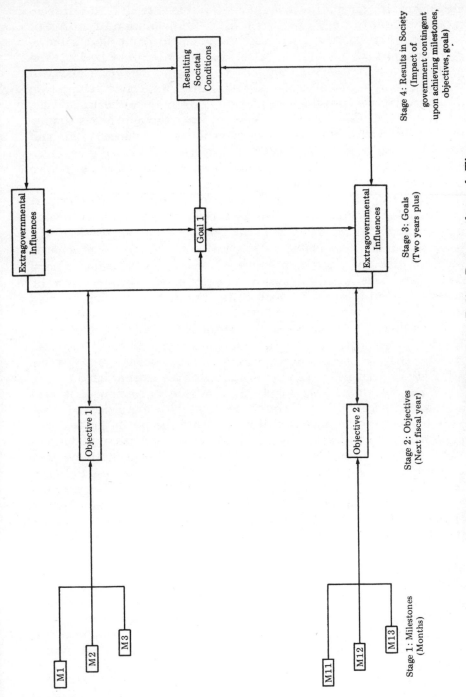

**FIGURE 6.1. A Simple Model of the Policy Process through Time**

appointment of a committee to prepare the report is a milestone. Objectives are targets for achievement within a twelve- to eighteen-month period. In some cases, such as the implentation of an Act of Congress, there will be a statutory requirement compelling achievement within that time frame. Fiscal year objectives may be complete in themselves; additionally they may be means to long-term goals.

Goals may be capable of realization in a finite time perspective, e.g., securing Congressional legislation for a national health service, or else reflect ideals to strive toward, even though, like a mathematical limit, they may never be reached, e.g., "a decent home and suitable living environment for every American." Virtually no Presidential objective is a "pie-in-the-sky" statement, but some involve much longer-term aspirations than others.

Departmental output is, in turn, often an input to another part of the federal government, such as the legislature. A department's long-term goal may be to achieve Congressional approval of the recommendation formulated as its fiscal year objective. The achievement of this goal is not, however, the same as changing societal conditions. This may be logically and empirically distinct from the achievement of a long-term goal. In the example of housing, enacted legislation will only be an input to a national housing market, which is also influenced by many other things outside the control of HUD. Insofar as government activities are meant to influence American society, they are best conceived as inputs to society, more or less influential according to the circumstances of the issue at hand.

While the diagram in Figure 6.1 and the discussion of it may appear complicated, it is a considerable simplification of what happens in reality. The analyst's distance from the policy process permits him to identify a lengthy chain of events, from the initial stimulus to the implementation of a policy. Those most involved tend to concentrate upon what is nearest at hand, reacting to inputs impelling them to action, and producing outputs that in turn are inputs to others in the process. An appreciation of the labyrinthine character of the policy process inspired MbO staff to try to improve the direction of policy by monitoring how quickly and in what direction the activities of different groups within a department led to identified objectives and goals. As Chapter 8 illustrates, OMB's ability to perceive the interconnectedness of different operating units reflected detachment from the hands-on position of line managers concerned with meeting immediate pressures and problems.

The MbO system operated in the federal government does not require officials to have a program design that is sure to get results, or that is even assumed to produce results. MbO documents concentrate upon actions that government can control; they are not meant to provide a causal model of all that is necessary to achieve a desired goal. Management associates accept that most long-term goals are likely to be influenced by things outside the control of the federal government. This is obviously the case with goals concerning the international economy, e.g., "reforming the international monetary system of the IMF." But it is also true of policies that involve the cooperation of state and local government. Even the cooperation of other departments within the executive branch cannot be taken for granted by a department enunciating objectives and goals. A series of management conferences in which a department reports to OMB that it has passed all its milestones is neither necessary nor sufficient evidence that it has achieved its objective. It is simply a statement that the department has done what it considers itself able to do to move in an agreed direction.

The uncertain cause-and-effect linkage between milestones, objectives, goals, and societal conditions does not vitiate the value of analysis. It could be argued that in conditions of uncertainty, it is at least as important to monitor the inputs that managers can control as it is to await evidence of achievements independent of government influence. By requiring milestones, supervisors have a means of monitoring whether line officials have succeeded in achieving tasks that, at a minimum, are not irrelevant to objectives. By linking milestones to calendar dates prior to the achievement of objectives, supervisors can also monitor whether departmental actions are moving according to schedule. If an achievement is not reached by a milestone date, then the responsible manager is expected to account for the variance, and to indicate when the action will be accomplished, and whether the delay is of minor or major significance in reaching the objective. Because program managers are the men who specify milestones, they cannot dismiss tardiness in meeting their own standards as of no consequence.

There are many ways to cut into the policy process—as well as many points at which one can check out. An academic contemplating social problems in a university may look far into the future and across a broad span of extragovernmental as well as governmental influences; the housing market in the mid-1980s or American society in the year 2000 may be the social condition constituting the final output in an academic scheme of analysis. By contrast, a low-level bureaucrat will be concerned with only a few things that are part of a single milestone action. The existence of multiple perspectives and time frames makes it confusing to speak of the results of a government policy, as if they were a once-for-all achievement. Because one man's results are an input to yet another cycle of activity, there can be no simple stipulation of performance measures or milestones for monitoring the policy process. There can only be a sequence of measures for a series of results.

The MbO system concentrates most attention upon what happens in the first stages of the policy process. In the course of an annual cycle, management associates monitor departmental activities by keeping track of the achievement of milestones. This substitutes concentration upon immediate action inputs of a department for uncertainty about achieving long-term goals or objectives. In a small proportion of instances, the cause-and-effect relationship between milestones and achievements is almost mechanical in its certainty; that is, if you do A, B, and C, then X will happen (e.g., constructing a dam). More often, the milestones represent all that a department can do, without certainty of success, in efforts to achieve immediate objectives or in hopes of advancing toward longer-term goals. For example, Commerce Department objectives to increase American exports and foreign tourist visits to America cannot be achieved solely by departmental actions. Milestones record actions that the department *can* control, e.g., trade promotion fairs, opening offices abroad to promote exports and tourism, and actions to encourage more effort by companies engaged in export or tourism. Similarly, any departmental objective that refers to lawmaking accepts that what the department can do is a less important determinant than Congressional action.

In the management-by-objectives system, the first step is achieving milestone actions. Table 6.1 classifies the different types of.

**TABLE 6.1. Types of Milestone Actions within Government**

|  | 1974 | | 1975 | |
|---|---|---|---|---|
|  | N | % | N | % |
| Organizational effort (Existing laws, funds, and personnel are redirected by bureaucratic efforts to achieve objective) | 117 | 49 | 111 | 49 |
| Evaluation (Review a problem and make a policy recommendation) | 63 | 27 | 48 | 21 |
| Lobbying Congress | 28 | 12 | 15 | 7 |
| Money (Spending funds or cutting expenditure as the primary means of action) | 6 | 2.5 | 7 | 3 |
| Resource change (Altering the physical or built environment, or utilizing new technology) | 9 | 4 | 9 | 4 |
| Negotiation (talk with agency having something to exchange) or exhortation (talk with nothing to exchange) | 7 | 3 | 30 | 13 |
| Means unspecified | 7 | 3 | 5 | 2 |

action inputs that departments specify as means to their objectives. Nearly half (49 per cent) of all departmental actions are organizational, involving the redirection of efforts of existing staff, without new legislation or appropriation. This is consistent with OMB's wish to avoid management objectives becoming a device for departments making demands for resources that can be processed through the budget or State of the Union message. In one-quarter of cases, a department commits itself to think about a policy by a formal evaluation of a problem. While in the short term this may delay action, it can also be viewed as a preliminary to legislation, appropriations, and new programs. This interpretation is supported by the fact that the promotion of new legislation by Congress is third in frequency of mention in 1974. The chief difference in the milestone actions in the first and second year arises from the fact that OMB wished to remove Congressional lobbying from the MbO system on the assumption that the departments and the White House would never overlook such objectives. Negotiation looms larger in the second year because of the submission of State Department objectives for the first time. Fifteen of State's nineteen objectives could only be achieved through negotiations with foreign powers.

As there are strict limitations upon the extra funds or new legislation that a department can hope to secure in a given year, it is realistic for departments to concentrate upon actions for which they retain the initiative. In four-fifths of all cases, the milestone actions are well within the control of the department proposing them. Only if lobbying Congress, changing the environment, or negotiating with others is involved need a department worry that it may not be able to pass the first milestones in the achievement of its objectives. Even then, it can take necessary preliminaries, e.g., commissioning engineering studies or arranging talks intended to produce successful negotiations or changes in Congressional views. Milestone statements are invariably actions that can be commenced within a matter of weeks or months. In nine-tenths of cases, departments and OMB overseers can ascertain with a reasonably high degree of reliability whether or not milestones have been achieved. Five-sixths of the milestone actions require only a marginal adjustment of existing departmental activities, rather than the establishment of new procedures or organizations as a precondition of progress.

From a departmental perspective, it is likely to be easier to achieve objectives kept within a department, or even better, within a bureau. Moving from initial actions to achieving objectives is then a matter of progress chasing within an agency. While this may not be easy, it at least avoids the complexities of interagency, executive-legislative, or intergovernmental relationships. If this point is taken to its logical conclusion, the ideal objective would hypothetically be something such as "reorganize data-processing facilities in the Bureau of Standards." Yet objectives that concern only activities within a department are of little or no concern to those outside. In about one-third of the cases, milestone actions are inputs to the same department. In another third, a department's milestone actions are inputs to other parts of government elsewhere in the executive branch, Congress, or state and local government.

To monitor progress presupposes that one can determine whether or not milestone actions and objectives have been achieved. This presents little difficulty in the elucidation of milestones; they are usually stated in precise rather than vague form and concern actions controlled by the department proposing an objective. There is no incentive for a department to put forward an objective for Presidential endorsement if it cannot think of ways to move toward it, however small the steps may be. Within a given department, the clearly stated milestones make for ease in scheduling work and, equally important, for ease in discharging responsibility. A particular operating unit can reckon that it has achieved *its* objective, when a milestone for which it is responsible has been reached without regard to its significance for the realization of an objective.

Identifying the achievement of an objective is much more difficult. Insofar as objectives refer to conditions outside the immediate control of bureaucrats, then they concern relatively remote and, conceivably, less well-defined objectives. Insofar as lower-level career officials regard the MbO system as a threat to their autonomy, or as an attempt to record their failures as well as successes, then such officials have an incentive to produce vague, ambiguous, or confusing statements, so that it will be impossible to show that an objective has not been achieved.

OMB recognized the crucial importance of measuring success in its initial circular. It asked departments to identify objectives in terms allowing subsequent verification of accomplishment. Verification does not require quantification—contrary to statements often made by proponents and detractors of management by objectives. It requires reliability, that is, a reasonably high probability that several persons, each independently observing a set of government actions, would give the same judgment about the achievement (or non-achievement) of an objective. Reliability does not ensure the validity of an assessment; agreement can result from group cohesion, or from a common self-interest in proclaiming success. In a political context, if all observers agree, this is good enough for practical purposes.

In the first two years of the MbO system, the achievement (or nonachievement) of one-quarter of Presidential objectives could be assessed in a highly reliable manner. Most of these easily verified objectives were achievements involving laws, e.g., whether a bill had been passed, or subject to audit-type verification, e.g., whether a new building has been constructed or a departmental committee has produced a set of recommendations. Quantitative objectives, such as targets for reducing expenditure, were relatively few. Almost half the objectives have been capable of fairly reliable assessment, that is, there is a better than 0.5 probability that different observers would agree in their judgment, but less than the almost certain probability of highly reliable measures. Fairly reliable objectives involve the use of "soft" numbers, have vague assessment criteria, or are likely to invite dispute among evaluators. One-third of objectives in the first year and one-quarter in the second could only be verified with low reliability, because of vagueness in statement, e.g., the creation of an "integrated" management system, or controversy in definition, e.g., reducing welfare program abuses to a "minimum." The reduction in the proportion of very unreliable objectives in the second year indicates that such objectives may progressively be reduced by careful OMB scrutiny. It is unlikely, however, that the great bulk of objectives can be stated in a form permitting verification in highly reliable ways.

Management by objectives does not have a single goal, such as saving money or generating new laws. It is designed to accommodate objectives in many different forms—Acts of Congress, bureaucratic behavior, public expenditure, or in the lives of American citizens. As the initial OMB circular emphasized, "There are no limitations on the subject content of objectives. They may involve desired program accomplishments, issue and legislative development or major administrative reforms."

In total, 75 per cent of Presidential objectives for 1974 concerned achievements within the federal government. (Table 6.2) First and foremost are bureaucratic objectives, usually noncontroversial matters affecting the personnel and procedures of government, e.g., HUD's objective "to assimilate the Office of Emergency Preparedness's disaster functions pursuant to Reorganization Plan No. 1." Second in frequency are objectives realized by deciding what future course of action to recommend. For example, HEW's ultimate objective is to find a cure for cancer. In the 1974 fiscal year it concentrated upon preparing a Cancer Program Strategic Plan to recommend what the next steps in cancer research ought to be. The passage of new legislation ranks third in significance because of the uncertainties of Congressional adoption of departmental policies. (Even in a British-type parliamentary system, where the government normally has an assured legislative majority, the passage of a major measure can require at least two years, one for drafting the bill and another to see it through the procedural stages of both houses of Parliament.) In the Nixon Administration, public expenditure objectives concerned more efficient use of existing funds, rather than paying out more money. For example, the Small Business Administration had as an objective "reducing the rate of delinquencies and projected loss rates for non-disaster loans by ten per cent." Presidential objectives took much the same form in 1975. The drop in the proportion of "within government" objectives from 75 to 64 per cent is in part technical: no international objectives of the State Department were included in the first year's figures.

Presidential objectives referring to achievements in the world outside Washington take disparate forms. (Table 6.2) In 1974, the most frequently cited "external" objectives refer to changes in the physical environment, e.g., the AEC's wish to "demonstrate the

TABLE 6.2. The Forms of Presidential Objectives

|  | 1974 | | 1975 | |
|---|---|---|---|---|
|  | N | % | N | % |
| A. Within government | | | | |
| Bureaucratic (affects personnel, procedures of government) | 75 | 32 | 67 | 30 |
| Report (Recommendations of a policy review or study group) | 62 | 26 | 44 | 20 |
| Legislation | 26 | 11 | 17 | 8 |
| Public Expenditure | 14 | 6 | 16 | 7 |
| Subtotals | | 75 | | 65 |
| B. Outside government | | | | |
| Physical change in material environment, resources (e.g., space shuttle, energy supplies) | 21 | 9 | 26 | 12 |
| Economic system (affects a complex set of economic relations, e.g., wage-price stability) | 20 | 8 | 19 | 8 |
| Economic contract (concerns specifiable actions by formal organizations) | 5 | 2 | 8 | 4 |
| Social system (affects complex social relations, e.g., utilization of health services) | 7 | 3 | 2 | 1 |
| Social categories (concerns specified groups of people, or individuals, e.g., AFDC mothers) | 7 | 3 | 10 | 4 |
| International system | (not applicable) | | 16 | 7 |
| Subtotals | | 25 | | 36 |

scientific feasibility of controlled thermonuclear fusion." The only other frequently mentioned set of objectives concerned improvements in the economic system, both at home and internationally. In 2 per cent of cases, specific firms or industries are the target of government actions. Only 6 per cent of objectives refer to government efforts to help specific groups of people, e.g., miners suffering from black lung disease, or to improve the social system, e.g., reduce crime. The increase in concern with the world out there in 1975 does not reflect an increase in social concerns, but rather greater attention to physical energy resources.

The great majority of government departments concentrate the great majority of their objectives upon matters within the confines of government itself, rather than reaching out to impact the world outside Washington. Even HEW, a department nominally concerned with social conditions, states most of its objectives in the form of bureaucratic achievements, or the preparation of reports with policy recommendations. This reflects the fact that often HEW's outputs are inputs to other organizations, e.g., to Congress when new laws are required, or to state and local government in efforts to improve the management of existing programs. In 1974 Interior and the Environmental Protection Agency more often cited the promotion of legislation in Congress than objectives immediately directed at the country's natural resources. The agency most concerned with bureaucratic objectives is not the Civil Service Commission but the Defense Department. In the absence of a shooting war, the military concentrates efforts upon the organization of forces under its command. The ability to manage one's own troops and resources is a necessary condition for the effective use of armed forces against a foreign foe.

A dilemma facing public officials is whether to concentrate upon objectives immediately within their power to realize, or upon objectives with greater outreach. The greatest certainty of success is likely to occur when objectives are exclusively concerned with departmental matters. If a department cannot control its own actions to produce satisfaction (especially if the objective is vague, such as better management), there is little prospect that it can affect the world around it. But to do this is to assume that the purpose of a ship's voyage is to satisfy the crew, rather than to move people and goods somewhere. Objectives requiring cooperation from other institutions of the federal system, or from groups of people or economic groups outside government, run greater risks of frustration. But they also promise wider impact, because they affect other parts of society. The most ambitious objectives are those concerning delicately balanced relationships greatly affected by forces outside government control, like the international economic system.

A majority (51 per cent) of 1974 Presidential objectives could be achieved by unilateral actions within the federal government. An additional 11 per cent could be attained by intergovernmental bargaining between federal, state, and local institutions, e.g., the implementation of new revenue-sharing programs, and 4 per cent by bargaining between governmental and nongovernmental organizations, e.g., issuing permits for construction of a Trans-Alaska Pipeline or leasing land on the Outer Continental Shelf for oil exploitation. In 1975, 64 per cent of Presidential objectives could be achieved unilaterally by the federal government, or by bargaining in which it was an important partner. The distribution of objectives within the foregoing categories was slightly different, but the aggregate proportion of government-dominated objectives was only 1 per cent less than in 1974.

When public officials define objectives in the economic or social system, they lose the prospect of certain achievement. Economic and social systems are autonomous processes, rather than formal organizations. One cannot sign a contract with an economic system, as one might with an oil company, or target resources at social processes, as one might target money at people with attributes entitling them to categorical benefits. For example, a Department of Transportation objective to give the transportation industry "the maximum flexibility to adapt to changing technological and market conditions" can only be achieved as the outcome (or by-product) of the partisan mutual adjustment of many different groups, some consciously concerned with influencing transport policy, and some only incidentally and accidentally impacting it. (Cf. Lindblom, 1965) The most that the federal government can do is to provide inputs to social and economic processes where extragovernmental determinants are also very important. Overall, 25 per cent of 1974 objectives and 30 per cent of 1975 objectives *cannot be accomplished by any organization*, public or private. They are the resultant of social and economic processes.

One way government officials may resolve their dilemma is to link fiscal year objectives, concentrating upon matters immediately within the control of a department, with long-term goals with greater outreach. In a sense, however, the fifth year of a five-year plan never arrives; it is always *mañana*. Moreover, such plans will be outside the time horizon of many officials, such as Congressmen elected for two years or a President elected for a four-year term. Objectives must identify what is immediately required in the next fiscal year, in order to influence program managers concerned with problems that are real and pressing. If, however, current actions are not directed at longer-term goals, then political leaders cannot carry out major measures requiring four years from the development of a departmental position through Congressional legislation, appropriation, and implementation. By subdividing efforts in time, as well as among organizational units, governors may cumulatively take advantage of the persistence of government actions, while recognizing that the immediate future is of first concern.

In the first year of the MbO program, nine of the nineteen participating agencies explicitly linked most of their statements of fiscal year objectives with longer-term goals. In the second year, one-third of agencies identified long-term goals. This reflects an apparent desire to tighten statements by concentrating upon problems of immediate concern. The great majority of statements of long-term goals are loosely coupled to fiscal year objectives. In other words, the achievement of an objective in the next year is not part of a comprehensive multi-year plan to achieve clearly identified results. Instead, it is one step in the right direction; subsequent steps in the years beyond are not identified. Exceptionally, a NASA or AEC engineering-type goal can involve a precisely articulated plan extending forward for several years. But even NASA can uncouple immediate objectives from goals. For example, the fiscal year objective "Complete testing for the proof test orbiter by September, 1974" is related to the long-term goal, "Increase scientific knowledge and understanding through exploration of the earth's environment, the planets and the universe," which could be realized (or fail of attainment) through a multitude of different action programs.

The absence of long-term goals in most departmental statements reflects a politically realistic calculation that long-term achievements are greatly dependent upon an ever-changing political environment. By stating varied objectives for a fiscal year about to commence, a department is spotlighting several measures that point in the direction that it wishes to go, and that it thinks are immediately capable of attainment. Further developments twelve months hence can be left to depend upon success in the coming months, not only in substantive terms, but also in terms of realizing or maintaining political support. A department's programs can only progress by increments if one year's actions lead somewhere beyond.

Because the management-by-objectives system directs agencies and OMB to review a year's accomplishments at the same time as the next year's list of objectives is being prepared, there is potentially a mechanism for monitoring continuity and change from year to year. By contrast with budgeting, in which a department normally starts by reaffirming the previous year's request for funds, the MbO system does not expect that a department will simply repeat its previous year's list of objectives. For a department to do this would be an admission that it had failed to achieve anything it had set out to do in the previous twelve months. A department has the following options: (a) introduce a new objective unrelated to any from the previous year; (b) introduce an objective that is a stage subsequent to an objective achieved in the past year; (c) repeat an objective from the previous year which is recurring or has yet to be accomplished; (d) omit an objective because it has been achieved; or (e) omit an objective because the department no longer wishes to move in that direction, or has no wish to give it a priority.

The annual review of objectives can thus be more like a "zero-based" review of priorities than the review of a budget in which pre-existing financial commitments are 90 per cent of all requests. The statement of objectives should normally involve discontinuities with the previous year or at least, different steps in a cumulative process. A department also retains the option of stopping a commitment. For example, if a Secretary does not like the look of policy recommendations prepared in pursuit of an MbO objective, he will not wish to make lobbying for Congressional enactment of the proposal an objective in the coming year.

Of the Presidential objectives approved for 1974, about half (53 per cent) were definitely part of a longer-term departmental program, for they show continuity with objectives proposed for 1975. Of 1975 Presidential objectives, about half (55 per cent) reflect continuity; 11 per cent are new because the State Department and FEA had not previously filed statements, and the remainder register new priorities in established programs. A typical example of continuity is the 1974 Interior objective of issuing a permit for the Trans-Alaska Pipeline. In 1975 it has the objective of providing government assistance to expedite the actual construction of the pipeline. In other instances, continuity gives departmental visibility to a recurring effort. In 1974 Agriculture wished to sell 11.8 billion board feet of timber from National Forest lands. In 1975, it wishes to sell another 11.8 billion board feet. Few 1974 objectives are repeated a second year because of failure of accomplishment, except when a department fails to get a bill through Congress, and wishes to try again another year. The elimination of a concern usually reflects successful completion of a short-term objective (e.g., the implementation of a new Public Law), or else a shift in OMB priorities, relegating a measure from Presidential status to the level of a departmental or bureau chief objective.

The typical Presidential objective involves one limited step toward a desired goal. But the same could be said about most political activities—whether involving the executive branch, Congress, or parties and pressure groups. The time required to realize any policy intention, except in an emergency, is likely to be measured in five- or ten-year units in a government as complex as that of the United States, and in a polity where so many different interests compete for government benefits. While the steps registered in Presidential objectives may not be sufficient to get you there from here, they nonetheless illustrate what has to be done first, by starting from where you are.

# 7

# "Tracking Together"

*Each successive fad is believed during the period of its popularity to be capable of solving all of the problems of the federal government. The fads originate from real problems and real solutions, but the Bureau (of the Budget) pounces on something that has worked somewhere and extrapolates universal principles. Then things come unstuck when they take it to the agencies.*

Departmental program manager

Introducing a new idea into an organization with as much inertia as the federal government immediately brings enthusiasts down to earth. A novel idea may collapse on impact with reality, as in the case of PPBS, because the organization is said to be not good enough for the concept. Or it may succeed, as in the creation of the Bureau of the Budget, because political leaders and institutional innovators accept the world as it is as their point of departure. The promoters of MbO first of all needed to influence officials who have been governing the country for years without MbO, in order to get their ideas permanently institutionalized.

The documents that are the immediate and visible output of the management-by-objectives system are a start, not the goal. Management by objectives is intended to produce action. Action require actors. The MbO staff does not act alone; it interacts with many other players within the Executive Office of the President, and in each department. In analyzing the effort to institutionalize MbO, one must first consider its relations with officials already in place before MbO came on the Washington scene to see whether and how they are "tracking together."

The introduction of yet another new division and yet another acronym within OMB was greeted with hostility, suspicion, jealousy, and scepticism by a significant number of old-line Bureau of the Budget staff. Inquiring reporters had no difficulty in finding critics within OMB; they normally preferred to be anonymous because, as one put it, "This Administration likes people to be loyal." (Havemann, 1973: 792) There was hostility from examiners who asserted that the way ahead for OMB was to return to the Bureau of the Budget's *modus operandi* back in the days before PPBS (and much else) came to their part of Pennsylvania Avenue. There was suspicion of the motives of the chief propagator of the system, Frederic Malek, because of his White House responsibility for personnel, at a time when career civil servants feared a Republican "purge" of the bureaucracy, notwithstanding Malek's own declaration of concern with upgrading public personnel. (Cf. Malek, 1974a and *Presidential Campaign Activities of 1972*) MbO not only brought Malek into OMB with his own staff, but also gave him lines of communication to departments where he had helped select new Assistant Secretaries for Administration and Management. There was jealousy because the new management associates tended to be well paid and self-confident, sometimes sporting symbols of business success. The claims of a few brash young men about what they and their system would do did not increase their popularity—especially when several demonstrated that the first thing it did was lead them to better government jobs outside the MbO system!

The professional perspective of many budget examiners encouraged scepticism of any management technique that was divorced from the budgeting process. Men concerned with money reacted to MbO initially as "a lot of baloney." In such circumstances, the best that management associates could initially expect from the main professional group within OMB was indifference, while they proved themselves and their new management technique.

The first priority of the MbO staff thus became to institutionalize itself within OMB. Management associates were assigned to program divisions of their own, parallel to but separate from the budget examiners' divisions. They were on their own in establishing themselves. The immediate need to establish MbO in the departments led the management staff initially to turn their back on OMB and face toward the agencies, where they found assured allies among MbO staff similarly seeking to establish themselves within their agency. They also had an action-forcing deadline mandated by the President and reinforced by a directive from the head of OMB: the preparation of objectives for fiscal year 1974, ten weeks from the initial request for action.

Of the four management divisions, that devoted to Economics and Government gave most attention to the specific problem of establishing MbO. Because its seven staff were stretched across seven agencies—Treasury, Justice, Commerce, Transportation, the Small Business Administration, the General Services Administration, and the Civil Service Commission—it was hard pushed to respond both to the claims for attention from those agencies that positively wished to make something of MbO, and from those clueless about what to make of MbO. By comparison, the division for National Security and International Affairs had only one "hopeless" department, State. Defense and the CIA were already organized to think in the analytic terms required by the MbO system. Colin Blaydon, the director of the management division for Human and Community Affairs, monitoring HEW, HUD, Labor, Action, and the Veterans Administration, took a different view of what his management associates could best do. This Harvard Business School economist reckoned it best to invest his staff's time primarily in special analytic studies to develop new programs, or recommend major changes in established programs that were not working properly. The division concerned with Natural Resources, Energy and Science had hardly commenced work before the energy crisis broke. The staff quickly became involved in the "fire-fighting" activities thrust upon OMB prior to the creation of the Federal Energy Administration.

One indicator of the integration of management associates within OMB is that within a year of starting work, the staff were asking themselves "What business should we be in?" and giving disparate or ambivalent answers. Most management associates quickly developed a respect for the skills of budget examiners, their colleagues down the hall. They saw that examiners were dealing with problems that were real and immediate, whether in their nominal task of investigating the budget, or in ad hoc fire-fighting activities. In terms of prestige and priorities within OMB, this is where the action is. Because of their detachment from the work of examiners, management associates were able to ask whether this was where the action *ought* to be. They identified two tasks that budget examiners were not doing. The first—monitoring program implementation and the management of established but not necessarily satisfactory programs —complements the examiners' concern with questions of current and future choice in budget recommendations. It also fits readily within the terms of reference of the MbO system. In the words of one management associate overseeing program management, it involves "a more careful specification of what the policy is than an Act of Congress or budget appropriation can provide." The second task— preparing special analytic studies on topics as diverse as the future of military health care for civilians, or federal funding for higher education when current laws expire in 1976—could be done by budget examiners. Management associates stepped in because hard-pressed budget examiners usually do not have the three weeks or three months to invest upon a single special study. Management associates could do so because once established, supervising an MbO system is not itself a full-time task. Fred Malek regarded it as a half-time task; many individuals and some division heads put it at one-third or less. Management associates are thus free to move opportunistically where their efforts bring most influence and prestige within OMB.

Paradoxically, institutionalization may not strengthen management by objectives in OMB, insofar as management associates decide that their best way to make a mark is to concentrate attention upon special analytic studies, rather than upon the further development of the MbO system. The argument for doing so became particularly strong, once the initial MbO procedure had been established and its chief proponent within the agency, Fred Malek was replaced as deputy director by a former budget examiner, Paul O'Neill. Yet there are management associates who feel that this risks overlooking important management questions that the MbO system can surface.

Insofar as management by objectives is part of a process, management associates might be placed together with examiners in unitary program divisions. Many overworked examiners would gladly accept management associates as individuals, as they demonstrate knowledge of programs and bureaucratic skills. Their reassignment to examination divisions would increase the budget manpower available by one-seventh. Budget review, management, and special analytic studies for an executive branch department could then all be done by one enlarged division. The strongest proponents of management concerns tend to dislike merger, fearing, as one put it, "After six or eight weeks we would get sucked into the same firefighting activities as the examiners."

Establishing management by objectives within the Office of Management and Budget was the smaller half of the problem of institutionalizing it within the executive branch of government. OMB is, by the standards of Washington, a very small agency. Institutionalizing a new system in the departments is much the bigger half of any centrally planned innovation. From the viewpoint of the creators of MbO, this requires success in twenty-two departments. Establishing the system there is crucial for success, inasmuch as MbO is meant to influence the behavior of middle-level program managers, as well as OMB and departmental overseers. In order to do this, it is necessary for OMB staff to convince line managers and departmental staff that the MbO system is in the department's interest. Since each federal department and agency tends to have distinctive program responsibilities, clients, organizational features, and its own cadre of ever-changing Presidential appointees, the MbO system cannot slot into the same organizational structure in each agency. The following pages characterize the different ways in which MbO was launched in departments; subsequent chapters provide generalizations.

The Interior Department, as nearly as any, provides a normal account of the introduction of the MbO system. In 1973, the Secretary, Rogers Morton, had a Congressional rather than an administrative orientation. Effectively the top man in the department overseeing the MbO system was the Under-Secretary, John Whitaker. The operation of the system was located in the office of the Assistant Secretary of Management, separate from Program Development and Budget. Two and sometimes three men worked on introducing the MbO system within the department. Given small numbers and remoteness from the power centers of the department—whether defined as the Office of the Secretary or that of the bureau chiefs— the staff concentrated upon developing objectives concerned with significantly altering existing programs, implementing newly approved programs, or reviewing problems in order to work out a departmental position for the White House and Congress. The objectives tended to be medium sized, e.g., "Develop a five-year land acquisition plan for a Federal Recreation and Wildlife Preservation Program," or "Implement approved water resource principles and standards," and occasionally politically controversial, e.g., "Issue permit for the Trans-Alaska Pipeline" or "Take specific actions to involve Indian people in strengthening tribal government." What is medium size within a department is likely to loom large to the bureau responsible, and, conversely, appear relatively small from a White House perspective. By the second year of the system's operation, Interior staff were able to set out department objectives in a clear, succinct form, with a justification and milestones noted for each, and less important departmental objectives distinguished from Presidential-level objectives.

The progress of bureaus toward their objectives is monitored within Interior by periodic meetings between the Under-Secretary and assistant secretaries and responsible program managers. Whitaker was prepared to devote up to two or three days a month to chairing these meetings. They are not a forum for debate about controversial policy issues or a place for determining choices. Instead, they are an occasion when those immediately concerned with managing programs can report their problems and progress. Presidential appointees can ask questions, and indicate alterations in objectives arising from changes in the political climate. The existence of conferences is important, inasmuch as it establishes dates when program managers are expected to report progress toward objectives. The small MbO staff is responsible for preparing the departmental management conferences and checking, both informally and formally with program managers, about points that could come up in the discussions. The management staff see the system as focussed on the most important continuing programs of Interior, picking up each year those elements that are subject to change. It is thus meant to complement the interventions from the Secretary's office, or OMB fire-fighting in a crisis situation. Department officials reckon that the system provides a suitable way of routinely keeping in touch with a sprawling and complex set of departmental responsibilities that will inevitably be run by those with "hands-on" control, but should be subject to periodic oversight by the Presidential appointees nominally responsible for them.

The Departments of State and Justice have proven inhospitable to the introduction of management by objectives, because they have been headed by major political figures who have seen their Cabinet post as a base from which to act as Presidential advisers rather than departmental administrators. Moreover, neither the diplomats in the State Department nor the lawyers who provide the backbone of staff in the Justice Department are trained or accustomed to look at problems as economists, systems analysts, or management scientists do. The introduction of MbO came at a particularly awkward time in the Justice Department, shortly after the assistant attorney general for administration was forced out following President Nixon's re-election and two weeks before Attorney-General Richard Kleindienst was forced to resign because of his activities in that campaign. In the autumn, the new Attorney-General, Elliott Richardson, also resigned, because of the President's activities in covering up activities in the campaign. The Justice Department was nonetheless able to put on paper a clear, succinct statement of objectives, justification, and milestones in the first year. Its problem was that Presidential appointees in the Justice Department usually had their minds on other things. MbO statements did not have support from the top necessary to give them force in operating programs. A Justice Department official who wished to remain anonymous told an inquiring journalist in November, 1973: "Nobody is doing anything differently than they used to because of the President's goals. People around here are worried about a lot of other things before they're worried about Presidential objectives. Nobody really cares about what the White House is hot for these days." (Havemann, 1973: 1704)

The State Department has a major continuing problem in identifying and achieving objectives: it can only act in relation to other sovereign states, which have objectives and goals of their own. It cannot, like the General Services Administration, hope to control its operating environment to a substantial extent. A second problem arises from the vague, general nature of many foreign policy goals, e.g., *detente.* The activities of the State Department that have proven suitable for MbO statements, such as the distribution of passports and visas, are least important politically among its activities. The status of the Secretary of State is such (particularly after Henry Kissinger took the post in September, 1973) that he has continuing contact with the President personally about the country's foreign policy objectives, and problems in achieving them. A Secretary of State would not report to the President via a management conference organized by the Director of OMB. In the second year of the program, the State Department made token compliance with the OMB request. The Under-Secretary of State for Political Affairs, Joseph J. Sisco, submitted fifteen themes concerning the remaining thirty months of the Administration. The themes concentrated upon such general, difficult to verify concerns as "security," "Atlantic partnership," "reducing the danger of hostility in the Middle East," etc. The introduction to the document aptly captures the vagueness and pious language in which each theme was diplomatically couched:

> No one nation can determine the course of the world. No other nation, however, can make a greater contribution to guiding the world in a positive direction. Our strength, our history, our moral vision compel an active American role.
>
> The central challenge before American foreign policy over the next thirty months or so that remain in this Administration is to help shape this open moment in history. The world can pursue one of two courses. We can turn to the days of narrow nationalism and competing blocs. Or we can take the path of collaboration.
>
> Our success in 1977 must be measured by the distance we have travelled down one of these two paths and the success we have had in setting a successful onward course for others to follow. We will be guided in large measure by these objectives.

There was nothing that management associates in OMB could do to make the State Department provide them with a more meaningful statement of objectives.

The outer Cabinet departments have many of the management problems of the departments closest to the White House, and fewer of the advantages. OMB's request to formulate Presidential objectives brought to the surface the uncertainties of many Presidential appointees about their responsibilities in the relatively short period of time in which they will be in a department. In the words of one such man: "You can't imagine how difficult it is for intelligent men to define what it is they're trying to accomplish. People here had presumed what they were doing was resulting in good. MbO forces you to define what you mean by doing good." (Havemann, 1974: 613) Moreover, departments such as Housing and Urban Development, Transportation or Labor are often concerned with national issues which are in no sense controlled or managed from their Washington office. OMB staff believe that the MbO system offers advantages to Presidential appointees in such agencies, for it simultaneously gives them a quick overview of the many things that were already going on before they joined the department—and will continue after they leave. In addition, it provides a means by which department heads can try to give some sense of continuing priority and visibility to the things that they may identify as their personal responsibilities in office. Inevitably, Presidential appointees differ, largely on personal grounds, in the extent to which they perceive management as a problem and wish to make use of this management technique.

The Department of Labor illustrates the experience of an old-line department away from the center of Presidential concerns. Shortly before the introduction of MbO, the Department had started to develop an internal progress-chasing system modelled after that in HEW. The Assistant Secretary for Administration and Management responsible for introducing the MbO system, Fred G. Clark, was a career civil servant experienced in Washington ways. The President's request to initiate an MbO system was not regarded as an imposition, but confirmation that the Department's earlier efforts were wise. The first year's statement of Department of Labor objectives concentrated on relatively big issues within the context of the Department: manpower reform, the work incentive program, occupational safety and health, compliance with minority hiring standards by federal contractors, etc. The form in which objectives were cast, however, tended to remove the awkward political points. For example, in occupational safety Labor intended "to achieve a fully coordinated integration of federal and state occupational safety and health programs." Achievements within the control of the Department were not clearly identified. In the second year, the statements of objectives had become much shorter and clearer, focussing upon the particular things that should (and usually, could) be done by Department of Labor officials. The Department's staff stressed a simple straightforward approach to monitoring progress within the department: "Progress will be monitored with a minimum of paper work. The system of accountability calls for the personal interaction between employees of successive levels of the Department, and the simple test of whether a scheduled event has been satisfactorily completed on time." A survey of the effect of the MbO system in the Department of Labor, based upon interviews with bureau chiefs as well as with assistant secretaries, concluded, "Clark's new guidelines are being followed closely at the top levels of the Labor Department, but they have not made much of an impact below the assistant secretaries." (Havemann, 1974: 616)

The General Services Administration and the Civil Service Commission are government agencies that *a priori* would seem well suited to the introduction of management by objectives, because they undertake activities with counterparts in large nongovernmental organizations, and their staple products—personnel, buildings, and federal records—are relatively stable, and readily identified. The Civil Service Commission objectives include such things as "reform of the federal pay comparability process" and "accelerating the implementation of managerial and executive development programs." GSA objectives include such explicitly commercial targets as "Sell $450 million of excess stockpile materials and receive $600 million in cash receipts by June 30, 1975" and "Reduce energy consumption in GSA-controlled space and vehicles." The GSA statement of its second year's objectives is specially notable for clarity, comprehensiveness, and succinctness. Each objective is not only accompanied by a brief justification and set of milestones, but also by a statement of manpower and budget resources required, and a listing of its impact upon other parts of the agency, and other government departments. Some objectives raise questions of choice, or present major management challenges within agency terms. For example, GSA stated as an intention, "Prepare a draft report on future automatic data processing strategy in the federal government," and the Civil Service Commission announced it would "Identify the essential elements of successful labor-management relations programs." The relative suitability of MbO in such agencies is not a source of encouragement for proponents of the system, because they are politically among the least visible agencies in Washington, and also atypical.

Among established agencies, Defense is distinctive in having had an established Planning Programming Budgeting System (PPBS) in place for a decade. PPBS, however, has emphasized future programs and choosing the most cost-effective program to achieve a given objective. MbO gives a different emphasis. The introduction of MbO to the Pentagon has drawn more attention to politically important issues that were not major spending issues, e.g., minority employment in the armed services and in defense industries. It has given more attention to questions of implementation (e.g., how and when will we carry out this choice?) and performance (e.g., how many military installations were painted with the money we authorized for maintenance a year ago?) The MbO approach focuses upon the accomplishment of agreed activities, e.g., "Improve the world-wide military command and control system (WWMCCS) and its information support," or the development of means conducting established activities better, e.g., "Improve the capability of the weapons acquisition process to assess proposed defense systems against their cost." This emphasis complements, and therefore adds something to the emphasis upon choice in PPBS. MbO objectives are selected at the start of the department's fiscal year and not, like PPBS statements concerning the budget, reviewed twelve to eighteen months before Congressional appropriations come into effect. The MbO system thus emphasizes current concerns that political leaders can immediately try to do something about. Given mammoth size and a command hierarchy with no equivalent in civilian agencies, the MbO system offers the principal officer involved, the Deputy Secretary for Defense, a chance to communicate better the priorities of the Office of the Secretary. In the words of one Pentagon official: "In DoD the problem is less that of making sure line officers are on the right side than it is of making sure that they are on the right wave length. It's formalizing a list of things to do. In a Department this size, you never can be sure if the people below you know what you want them to do." MbO communications and conferences between the Office of the Secretary and bureaucratically remote officials provide an additional means by which political leaders can try to give *de facto* weight to their *de jure* formal authority. OMB regard it as a sign of successful institutionalization that Defense officials in the Army, Navy, and Air Force have asked for assistance to establish MbO operations within these branches of the department, thus bringing the system closer to managers with hands-on operating authority.

The National Aeronautic and Space Administration is an established agency with considerable experience in systems engineering identification of long-term goals, e.g., putting a man on the moon and getting him back. NASA staff are fortunate in that their objectives are easily verified in physical terms, unlike the social goals of HEW. Moreover, because any major NASA project requires at least several years to accomplish, its staff have had to think in terms of milestones, fiscal year objectives, and long-term goals. Thus, NASA found OMB's request for a statement of objectives easy to meet, for it was being asked to report on what it was already doing. It is the engineering goals of NASA, rather than the "scientific" outlook of the agency, that has made it easy for NASA to produce MbO statements. The National Science Foundation's statements of Presidential objectives are described as "mushy even by the standards of social work."

Two agencies—Agriculture and Commerce—have sought to link their MbO system with the preparation of departmental budget requests. Such a step is consistent with the OMB belief, "Unless you move money, you haven't done anything."* In Agriculture, the MbO team already found in place a comprehensive statement of departmental programs prepared as part of an ill-fated PPBS effort in the late 1960s. The project produced an analysis of departmental activities in terms of 11 missions and 300 program structures linked to specific organization units and responsible officials. Moreover, the department has no difficulty knowing what its political objectives are. Congressmen from rural areas write legislation and appropriations with relatively explicit direction about what the department's bureaus can and cannot do. An MbO official who came to Agriculture from another department noted, "Congress monitors us daily. They will know things before we do sometimes, and they will not hesitate to tell us what our objectives ought to be." The Assistant Secretary for Administration, responsible both for management and budget, utilized the established program structure to ask bureau chiefs to prepare for the Summer, 1974 departmental budget review a succinct statement of the objective for each program, as well as stating what it would cost in the coming year. The innovation has not produced major shifts in the base expenditure in the budget, but it has altered the way in which political leaders make discretionary budget decisions. Typically, it affects the fine turning of appropriations within a program, e.g., shifting from the purchase of new equipment to maintenance, or shifting expenditure between different programs concerned with the same broad mission goal. In previous years, bureau chief submissions, each with detailed justifications, have been passed to the Secretary, who cannot have enough expert knowledge to challenge most properly written justifications. In such circumstances, the Secretary could only make decisions by applying general rules of thumb. By forcing bureau chiefs to commit themselves to statements of program objectives, budget recommendations can be altered in accord with political priorities, an area in which the Assistant Secretaries are meant to be the experts. The addition of MbO to the budget review process has resulted in Assistant Secretaries being able to make far more discretionary budget choices themselves than in previous years. The statements of objectives generated by the department's budget process provide the basis for the department's own internal monitoring of objectives on a year-round basis. The distinctive feature of the MbO system in Agriculture is not the statement of objectives, but the way in which these statements are then used by Presidentially appointed staff.

*In the view of some management men this is a mistake, because a budget is a set of accounts, not an operating plan, the incremental nature of budgeting ignores priorities specific to a single year, and the time lag between departmental request and Congressional action may be greater than the months remaining to a political appointee in office.

In Commerce too, the department had already analyzed expenditures in terms of about 250 programs prior to the introduction of MbO. Exceptionally, Commerce had also tried to develop procedures for monitoring what bureaus did with their appropriations. After the MbO system was launched, the department developed a two-step strategy for identifying and monitoring departmental objectives. In the budget cycle, bureau chiefs are required to include statements of objectives and milestones with each of their budget submissions. Then, after budget decisions are made in Congress as well as in the department, the MbO group can monitor progress toward already agreed objectives, in terms of already identified milestones. In Commerce the link between budgeting and MbO is in using the budget to produce basic information important in the MbO system. In Agriculture, MbO statements are used to produce basic data for budget decisions. The difference between the two departments may be less a matter of organizational procedure than of political personalities. Agriculture Secretary Earl Butz is much readier to face up to controversial decisions than Frederick Dent at Commerce. In both departments, the identification of objectives, like the budget process itself, begins with the bureau chief, rather than the Secretary.

A new agency such as the Environmental Protection Agency or the Federal Energy Authority has two basic problems: (1) What objectives, powers and resources can it claim in competition with other federal agencies, some of which may have opposed its foundation, or seek to annex some of its nominal responsibilities? (2) Who is in charge within the agency? These questions of power must be settled *before* management by objectives can be institutionalized. MbO is useful to those with power; it is not a means of conferring power upon officials who have yet to demonstrate that actions should follow from their words.

The Federal Energy Administration began in April, 1974 with an uncertain status vis-a-vis established agencies with energy concerns, such as Treasury and Interior; a director, John Sawhill, whose influence had yet to be tested against that of William Simon and Rogers Morton; and a staff that had never worked together before. The MbO group within FEA, recruited principally from HEW, saw the need for promptly providing the Administrator, Assistant Administrators, and their subordinates with reasonably clear and specific statements of what should be done in the immediate future. Former HEW officials reacted against the elaborate paperwork of that department's MbO system. Their motto became, "Replace paper with people." With Sawhill's backing, in reiterative discussions with him and his assistant administrators, the group identified forty-five agency objectives within two weeks. The system was promoted among assistant administrators as a means of getting the top man's commitment to their particular priorities, and using management conferences to gain his assistance in breaking bottlenecks. It was recommended to Sawhill as a means of learning about the chief concerns of his staff, and ensuring follow-up action on measures agreed in management conferences. Within six months, there was an MbO system in place in the Federal Energy Administration, but its utility was in question. During the same period, Sawhill had lost battles with competing agencies for major energy responsibilities and he shortly thereafter was fired by the White House. The MbO system was temporarily without a client, and the objectives and influence of FEA were in suspense.

In the Environmental Protection Agency, founded in 1971, management by objectives was introduced prior to the OMB initiative, and operated in a more stable political environment, at least initially, than FEA. The political forces that lobbied through the creation of the EPA were ready to support it in carrying out its mission, and regarded EPA as their chief agency. Statutory duties of regulation gave officials a clear sense of what they had to do immediately, and the powers they might invoke. Unlike OEO or HEW, the Environmental Protection Agency deals with problems that can be subjected to engineering technology. There was thus a reasonable basis for believing that the achievement of immediate fiscal year objectives, e.g., the determination of pollution control regulations, would lead to long-term goals, e.g., cleaner water or air. With well-defined agency powers and a reasonably stable leadership, the deputy administrator, Robert Fri (1974), was able to establish fiscal year objectives directed toward long-term goals of the fledgling unit. To assist in gaining attention from scattered regional managers and officials employed by pre-existing units amalgamated in EPA, Fri had the power to apportion budgets after Congressional appropriations, a matter of considerable importance in a new agency, where the base line for budgets has itself not been institutionalized.

In a political analysis, the identification of agency objectives inevitably receives the most attention. But MbO staff spend more time in monitoring progress that is (or is not) being made toward the agency's current annual objectives than in defining objectives. Such activity seems routine only to those who believe that government agencies can (or will) carry out automatically whatever has been chosen as their chief objectives. In a political environment in which White House staff are uncertain whether departmental officials are their collaborators or adversaries, it is politically prudent to monitor progress that ought to be routine to ensure, in a phrase characteristic of the Nixon White House, that "everyone is tracking together."

Management conferences—within each department, and between each department and OMB—are the chief mechanism for reviewing whether or not a department is making satisfactory progress toward its agreed objectives. Departmental management conferences normally have the Secretary or the Under-Secretary in the chair to receive reports from bureau chiefs and program managers and the assistant secretaries or equivalent staff overseers. The agreed list of departmental objectives constitutes the agenda for discussion. Subordinates thus have a clear idea of what they are expected to report about to their superiors. In turn, the Secretary has a list of priority items, chosen after some reflection, rather than on an ad hoc basis, and remaining the same throughout the year. This is particularly important if a new Secretary takes over in the middle of a fiscal year. He can use the MbO system to brief himself about what is going forward already in his department. The advantages of stability and predictability are not to be valued lightly in a political environment in which there are always momentary crises crying for attention. In the words of an Assistant Secretary of Labor:

> Government is a firehouse; you put out one fire and three more break out behind you.
>     It's nice to be able to keep your eye on something for a longer time, and MbO lets you do that. (Havemann, 1974: 616)

Periodic management conferences give a department's small MbO staff its chief routine responsibility—and its primary justification for informally monitoring line activities on behalf of the Office of the Secretary. Prior to each management conference, the MbO staff reviews, with liaison staff in the bureaus, the scheduled objectives assigned to the participants. In the words of one MbO staffer:

> We avoid asking people how well or badly they are doing. We are not handing out report cards. Instead, we ask: How are you doing? We want to know whether they are having problems, as well as successes. If they have problems, maybe the Secretary can help. What we really want from the bureaus is honesty about what's happening in their work.

For each objective on the agenda, responsible managers are expected to report whether the milestones due have been reached; if delays have occurred, what steps have been taken to overcome the difficulties; and, if circumstances have changed, whether they think the objective itself should be modified. MbO staff are quick to point out that program managers can use the management conference to enlist the support of the Secretary in breaking bottlenecks, for the objectives are a commitment by the Secretary, as well as his subordinates, to achievement. Most departmental management associates make a point of sending program managers as well as the Secretary their background paper prior to a management conference. In this way, management associates have to assure program managers that they are not seeking to second guess managers or act as a spy for the Secretary.

Because managers know that they will be periodically requested to report progress to their superiors, they have an incentive to achieve milestones by the date of a meeting. Because conferences are recurring, with the same agenda items under review, they have an incentive to report problems at an early stage, rather than concealing difficulties until failure is public. Because the agenda of objectives is limited in number and normally fixed through the year, managers have notice of what will be left to their own discretion, outside the Secretary's purview.

MbO staff are not encouraged to judge their work by the number of milestones that are achieved, or by the problems that are surfaced at an early stage. They are less concerned with producing elaborate progress reports on paper or lengthy analytic or advisory papers about departmental problems than they are with flashing green lights indicative of progress, or simple red and yellow warning signals. Moreover, their relatively junior status gives them little personal political weight. When they gain attention, they are expected to speak briefly and to the point; they do not enjoy roving commissions that characterize personal assistants in the Office of a Secretary.

The small full-time MbO staff are not meant to be fire-fighters, rushing to take over management tasks when difficulties arise. Instead, they are meant to stimulate achievement, periodically sending our reminders that, in a few weeks time, the Secretary or the Under-Secretary will be asking about progress that managers have made since their last conference. In the words of one management man, "While things don't get done differently, an awful lot of things get done more quickly than might otherwise happen, when people are reminded that they are soon going to have to say how well they are doing."

The conduct of departmental management conferences varies enormously, according to the status and personality of the man in charge. If the Secretary delegates the task of chairing the meeting to his Under-Secretary, this will signal to those who have not already noticed that he has little interest in keeping informed about many activities of major importance to bureau chiefs and assistant secretaries. Only an Under-Secretary known to have the personal confidence of a Secretary can speak with substantial authority. The chairman's personality and interest in departmental activities will greatly influence the extent to which subordinates make a management conference a dialogue in which information and ideas are exchanged in a more relaxed manner than in the adversary circumstances of a departmental budget review. Such discussions can give an isolated program manager his best or only opportunity to get some idea of what his Secretary feels about his unit's work—and also to influence the Secretary's feelings by reporting his aspirations and difficulties.

Management conferences are meant to involve more than inspirational talk. MbO staff men normally take minutes of discussions and list action items arising from them. Preparations for the next meeting can thus include a check that actions have followed minuted decisions, as well as refer to annual statements of objectives. For example, in one agency, ten management conferences in six months produced ninety action items, of which eighty-three were promptly implemented. The figures were compiled by management staff anxious to show the agency head the return he was getting for his investment of time in the meetings.

Within OMB, there is little incentive for management associates to invest time in continuous monitoring of departmental progress toward objectives. Management associates do not have the authority to act as program overseers, nor do they have the inclination. If a manager is having difficulty in making progress toward a Presidential objective, it is his responsibility or that of his departmental overseer to solve the problem, or to notify OMB if matters are more serious. Management associates can invest their discretionary time in special analytic studies focussed upon long-term improvements in departmental work, or go where the action is in OMB, by joining examiners in fire-fighting operations.

Management conferences between a departmental Secretary and the Director and/or Deputy Director of OMB are used to keep OMB routinely informed about progress toward Presidential objectives— and to make sure that departments realize that OMB detachment from day-to-day management problems does not mean that it has lost interest in results. In preparation for a management conference, OMB management associates go over the list of Presidential objectives and milestones with departmental staff to identify progress and problems, and prepare an agreed agenda for discussion between the Secretary and the Director. External audit requires that a department maintain its MbO system sufficiently to merit periodic inspection. It also requires the Secretary to be briefed within the department about the progress that line managers are making toward their Presidential objectives.

There are wide differences of opinion about the value of the high-level discussions that follow from these preparations. The discussions are valuable for a relatively unimportant non-Cabinet agency, because they give the agency head a chance to talk with the Director of OMB about major ongoing activities of the agency:

"Otherwise, we would only see him at parties, or in the adversary circumstances of the budget review." In the case of Defense, which has direct lines to the White House, the meetings provide an opportunity for the Director to focus on management problems of Defense, within OMB's area of concern, which might otherwise be ignored by an agency that puts military strategy and military hardware first. Criticisms of the conferences tend to focus on their size, their formality, and the tendency to concentrate upon generalizations. Because the two principals—the Secretary and the Director— are both several removes from line management, there is always the possibility that a manager can report what he thinks his supervisors wish to hear, rather than what he considers most important. In the words of one line manager, "OMB likes what we tell them, but frankly, we give them a lot of crap." In the words of another:

> It's like King Arthur's Round Table. There are 30 or so people gathered around, and everything is very ceremonial. The Assistant Secretaries stand up and give lecture after lecture about their objectives. Because they are very broad and general, what they say isn't always very meaningful. What they are really doing is asking for pats on the head. It's hard to get down to specifics in such a meeting, and impossible to raise awkward issues, especially when the department itself is deeply divided about what to do.

The variable extent to which the MbO system has been institutionalized within executive branch departments can be accounted for by the following five factors:

1. *The extent to which staff oversight of program management was institutionalized within a department* prior to *the introduction of the MbO system.* At one extreme, HEW had an MbO system already in place prior to the OMB initiative, albeit called by a different name, the Operational Planning System. At the other extreme, in new agencies such as ACTION or departments with complex responsibilities and a poor management history, such as Transportation or HUD, MbO staff had to provide the essentials of a system from scratch. In Defense, a PPBS-type review was part of the department's annual operating cycle. Management by objectives simply had to demonstrate how it could complement or supplement its work. Agriculture and Commerce illustrate one useful inheritance from the days of PPBS: the definition of departmental activities in terms of programs linked with operating units within the department.

2. *Political support from the top of the department.* If neither the Secretary nor the Under-Secretary in a department is interested in monitoring progress toward departmental objectives, this fact is soon made evident to program managers during periodic management conferences—or by the cancellation of such conferences. In such

circumstances, there can be no departmental program, for MbO staff cannot be the recipients of reports from career officials greatly outranking them, nor does an Assistant Secretary for Administration have the rank to make other assistant secretaries and those under him report in a politically meaningful way.

3. *Institutional attributes of departments.* These influence the interest of Presidential appointees in the management of the activities under them. The vast size of Defense, as well as the long lead-time of technical projects there (an attribute shared with NASA) makes management a major concern of the Office of the Secretary. By contrast, the Secretary of State does not see his political status affected by the management of his department, but rather by what he does outside the department, in collaboration with the White House. Personal factors also influence the extent to which individual Presidential appointees make use of the MbO system. For example, James A. Lynn, unlike some predecessors, brought to HUD a desire to get a handle on the activities of his department, and found the MbO system useful in this respect. Elliott Richardson brought to HEW an unusual desire to communicate with staff at all levels in the department in a two-way exchange of influence, and used the management conferences of MbO for this purpose.

4. *The extent to which the activities of a department can have objectives that are reasonably verifiable, stable, precise, and important to the department.* In a formal sense, program managers and operating staff always know *what* they are doing, even if they are not sure *why* they are doing things. In order to have objectives to monitor, it is necessary to factor out global statements of ideals into statements that are sufficiently discreet to fix responsibility within an operating unit within a department. Ironically, this may be easier to do in a balkanized department such as Interior, where bureaus are concerned with unrelated activities, than in State, where the overriding concern is an international system with a high degree of interdependency. The extent to which objectives can be measured or verified differs greatly between such agencies as NASA or the AEC, and HEW. HEW has met the problem by substituting process-type objectives (i e , the completion of a report, or implementing a law) in order to have something tangible to focus its management efforts on. In Agriculture, there may be debates about what the department should do, but there is a clear and steady awareness of *who* the Department should serve. Stability of goals or ideals is important, because this promotes bureaucratic appreciation of the significance of an objective, and ensures that Presidential appointees are not likely to change or reverse objectives every six months. The General Services Administration is an example of an organization with ex-

tremely stable objectives, whereas in State or Justice the emphasis in policy can swing back and forth between hard-line and soft views. Within an organization such as GSA, an MbO system can become significant inasmuch as it suits activities central to the mission of the agency. By contrast, within the State Department, an MbO system (or other analytic efforts, see, e.g., Mosher and Harr, 1970) cannot easily become significant, because it suits best activities peripheral to the chief mission of the department.

5. *The extent to which departmental officials perceive the MbO system as primarily benefitting their department, rather than the Office of Management and Budget.* This statement is, in a sense, a summary of preceding propositions: departmental staff will accept a system if they can believe that it makes sense to them. OMB's role is, in effect, to encourage departments to try out MbO. Without such a trial, the utility of the system cannot be demonstrated within the department. On the other hand, OMB sponsorship runs the risk of encouraging passive resistance, in the form of departmental staff disengaging from involvement. Within a department, there can be differences in the perceived advantage of the system, depending upon an individual's location. Inasmuch as MbO is intended to strengthen staff oversight, it is to be expected that staff and Presidential appointees will be quickest to see its potential usefulness to them. By the same token, line managers, receiving daily or weekly signals—by telephone or face to face—of what is going wrong with programs, as well as what is working, will have less use for a paper reporting system. Havemann (1974: 616) concludes: "If the experience of the Labor Department is any indication, management by objectives is catching on well at the upper levels of federal agencies, but not so well among career civil servants."

The MbO system is a means of circulating information and not a means of controlling the actions of bureaucrats. It is thus, first and foremost, a system that appeals to those who wish information. A cynic might say that people who wish information do so only because they lack power. But to assert this is to draw an overly rigid distinction between the two concepts. Information is a precondition for the intelligent exercise of power. A President who claims power without being informed about what is going on in the executive branch is no more than a puppet for those with their hands on action points. Yet those with information and no power cannot act upon their knowledge.

# 8

# Management by Whose Objectives?

---

*What a President does not know about the activities under way in Defense, State and CIA, to say nothing of the Office of Education and the Bureau of Indian Affairs is incalculable. There he sits, overworked and making the best of a bad situation, while all around him his princes and serfs are doing and undoing in thousands of actions the work of his administration without him having a clue.*

William D. Carey, Assistant Director,
Bureau of the Budget, 1969

*You can call them the President's objectives or you can call them the objectives of the Faery Queene. But if the department doesn't take them on board, then they are dead.*

OMB management associate

To institutionalize management by objectives as an active element in the policy process requires a client who wants the information that it can offer. A management technique that is only of interest to management specialists is a ritual device turning prayer wheels unconnected with the engines of government. One must not only ask what kind of a tool MbO is, but also whose tool is it?

Many of the 237 Presidential objectives for a year appear remote from the concerns of the White House. Few Americans would expect the President of the United States to give much time to "The establishment of a requirement that each agency initiate a manpower planning system within their overall agency management program." (Civil Service Commission) Nor would a decision maker be

117

expected to spend much time on a Department of Transportation objective to implement the 1973 Highway Act. A liberal critic of Richard Nixon's studied neglect of race relations would not expect him to include among his 1974 objectives the following Department of Labor target: "To increase employment opportunities for minorities and women by federal contractors and subcontractors and federally assisted construction contractors and subcontractors." The agencies most closely concerned with Presidential priorities, e.g., Defense, Treasury and Justice, contributed to the depoliticization of MbO statements as much as lesser agencies. Instead of submitting objectives concerned with matters that are the stuff of their frequent discussions at the White House, these departments used the MbO system to register lesser bureaucratic concerns.

In spite of the fact that the MbO system is intended to advance Presidential objectives, the White House has not been a significant client for the information that the system produces. The President has signed the call for departments to produce objectives, thus giving OMB authoritative support in its efforts to get response from the agencies. Presidential statements of policy, such as the State of the Union message, have provided a criterion to determine whether departmental objectives are inconsistent with White House wishes. Even before Watergate, President Nixon's disengagement from budget review and personal monitoring of domestic programs augured little Presidential use of the system. The resignation of John Ehrlichman and Robert Haldemann shortly after MbO was launched meant that there was no White House staff to assume the President's prerogatives.

President Nixon's personal contribution was confined to highlighting a few objectives of personal interest to himself, when sending back a blanket endorsement for departmental catalogs of the objectives of his Administration. For example, the President showed an interest in NASA's objective concerning links in space with Russia's SOYUZ spacecraft because of its foreign policy implications; he singled out the need to combat organized crime, when writing the Justice Department, and to encourage black capitalism when writing Commerce. In a letter to the Environmental Protection Agency, his emphasis upon maintaining economic growth as well as combatting pollution seemed to undercut the EPA mission. The second annual cycle of objectives was cleared through the White House at the trough of Presidential involvement in executive branch activities: the last weeks of the Nixon Presidency and the initial weeks of the Ford Presidency. The objectives were no different in substance than those cleared the previous year.

Whether the President would find it valuable to pay more attention to the MbO system is a matter of dispute among management associates. In the words of one senior OMB official: "The President has no idea in hell what is going on in this town. Because he only sees what hits him in the face, he thinks that the whole town is crisis oriented. He ought to know more about what is going on underneath him. He should take something like 50 to 75 objectives to focus on, and try to push action along." But another management associate saw a difficulty in closer Presidential involvement. It would mean a watering down of the specific content of MbO statements, because the President would not want to be personally committed to dozens and dozens of potentially trouble-making objectives. "An objective is a political commitment. With Presidential commitment you would have to start with objectives that are broad enough to mean all things to all people." President Ford has shown an appreciation of the need to monitor the performance of operating agencies, and also of the value of avoiding quick personal commitments to departmental objectives.

The Office of Management and Budget has not been the major client for the MbO system, notwithstanding the fact that it is supervised from within the agency itself. The most evident advantage that OMB enjoys is the addition of approximately thirty professionals to its program staff. This staff has been employed in many activities *outside* the MbO system. In particular, management associates have been used in "fire-fighting" tasks required by the ever-recurring emergencies that hit the Executive Office. In addition, management associates have contributed some staff time to special analytic studies of medium-sized federal programs in need of overhaul, when examiners have lacked the time or the inclination to become involved in such issues, e.g., the provision of a health care delivery system for families of military personnel, or occupational safety and health regulations.

Ironically, lack of interest in OMB has been most clearly, albeit unintentionally signalled from the top: the Director's office. The initial MbO plans envisioned bimonthly meetings between the Director and/or the Deputy Director of OMB and the head of each participating department. This effectively meant an OMB-management conference every other day in the working year. Within six months of launching the system, the Director's office of OMB was lagging far behind its planned timetable, notwithstanding the importance of these conferences in the plan for the system. Many conferences were cancelled during the autumn budget review. Meetings with agencies reporting to the Natural Resources and Energy Division were disrupted by the oil crisis. An agency with the visibility and vulnerability of EPA went five months without a conference, and Interior prepared for four meetings, only to have two cancelled at the last minute. The National Science Foundation, the least of the agencies involved, went more than six months without a meeting with OMB about its Presidential objectives.

OMB-department conferences have been no more frequent following the resignation of President Nixon. The transition at the White House was followed by a transition at OMB, with a period of marking time as Roy Ash resigned, to be replaced by James T. Lynn, former Secretary of HUD, and Fred Malek resigned, to be replaced by Paul O'Neill, promoted from within. In reviewing the MbO system, both men started from a basic working assumption: neither could commit himself personally to spend scarce time in frequent meetings with agency heads. One staff official facetiously suggested involving the President in such meetings. In that way, there would be no one who could pull the Director or Deputy Director away, causing a last minute cancellation! Yet without involvement from the top, there is no pressure on the Secretary to watch the progress within his department of management objectives, so that performance will be satisfactory when reporting to OMB.

The chief clients for the MbO system are the political appointees in the departments, starting with the Secretary or the Under-Secretary responsible for overseeing the activities of the department. About 90 per cent of the paper and dialogue generated by the system remains within the department concerned. The number of departmental objectives monitored is greater than the number of Presidential objectives, and the relationship between political overseers and line managers is closer than in the high-level (or, critics say, up in the clouds), staff-to-staff conferences between department heads and OMB. The Secretary has more of a personal stake in the identification of his department's objectives than does any outsider. Similarly, a bureau chief is sensitive to the evaluation placed upon his programs within the department and may hope for tangible recognition of success in the annual departmental budget review.

The MbO system provides the Secretary (and equally important, those in the Office of the Secretary) with information about the programs for which he is responsible. While the man on top likes to appear omniscient, the complexity of a government department and the brevity of his own appointment mean that he can only know a limited amount about what happens underneath him. The MbO system establishes routine reporting mechanisms about major departmental concerns. These objectives are then regularly and consistently monitored in management conferences. The preparation of the agenda reminds program managers that milestones are approaching and allows them, without any loss of face, to report difficulties in making progress; it is thus a "fire-prevention" rather than a "fire-fighting" technique, useful for averting crises rather than resolving them. In the hands of a Secretary or an Under-Secretary who is a good committee chairman, management conferences can be a forum for exchanging views about developments and shifts in emphasis within and between programs, and encouraging flexibility among both political appointees and program managers. The management conferences also ensure that those in attendance are fully briefed about a range of activities within the department, thus reducing the imperfections in the flow of information throughout the depart-mental hierarchy. The unobtrusive measure of communication of one attender at management conferences is simple: "I watch the Secre-tary's face. I've seen Secretaries learn things for the first time in these meetings. Their eyes show it." The flow of information to lower level appointees is also improved—both about what their colleagues are doing, and what is happening under them. An MbO staff man bluntly characterized an assistant secretary's reaction to management con-ferences thus: "He said he knew it all already, but I saw the bastard sitting there taking notes." Well-kept minutes recording actions agreed in the light of discussion can provide a basis for progress chasing by MbO or Secretarial staff, and thus follow through upon talk in management conferences.

One indicator of the usefulness of the MbO system to staff is that the majority of departments have responded to the Executive Office stimulus by instituting a program that involves more work and brings more information up to the Assistant Secretary for Administration, the Under-Secretary and, upon occasion, the Secretary, than is re-quired to conform to the vague minimum standards specified by OMB. Interviews suggest that in most departments the MbO system is sufficiently useful as a simple monitoring mechanism to survive within the department, even if OMB abandoned its central role, and made the use of management by objectives simply another technique that it was prepared to advise agencies about.

Bureau chiefs and line managers concerned with a single program are potentially the saboteurs rather than the clients of MbO, insofar as the MbO process is (or is perceived as) a means of strengthening the power of their political superiors over their actions. From the beginning, management staff have had to emphasize what the MbO system is *not*, in order to reassure suspicious line managers. Firstly, it is not a means of forcing objectives on line managers from the top down. Secondly, it is not intended to be a performance audit upon line managers, or to establish a contract specifying results for which they will be held responsible. Thirdly, it generates relatively little paper by federal standards; it is designed to short-cut lengthy written reports by management conferences. Fourthly, there are no sanctions to be brought against civil servants who fail to achieve objectives; an offsetting disadvantage is that there are few rewards that can be offered those who succeed in attaining the relatively routine and predictable things that constitute the bulk of MbO objectives.

The program managers at lower levels of the federal executive do not need an MbO system to provide them with information. Their routine responsibilities and position give them a steady flow of information about the progress of programs for which they are responsible. Collectively, the cluttered desks of these individuals provide a conspectus of how the executive branch of government is managing its greater and lesser responsibilities. Such information is nowhere collated. The point of the MbO system, and of much of the work of OMB, is to bring together such information on a selective basis, so that matters of concern to political appointees can quickly be brought to the attention of those formally responsible for giving direction to government. The rub is that one has to sort through much trivia, in order to find an occasional nugget of important information. Political appointees do not have the time or the knowledge to do such a sorting job. Bureau chiefs and line managers do this routinely for the programs for which they are responsible.

The participation of lower-level managers in management by objectives is a precondition of the system becoming operational. The MbO system has succeeded in becoming operational in most departments, no simple achievement in a world where new ideas are often evanescent as well. But the price of becoming quickly operational is that it has been made to work on terms acceptable to lower-level managers. These public officials have been less concerned with the use that they can make of the system than with the possible use that others can make of it against their interests. Line managers do not expect headquarters-based information to tell them more about what they are doing, but rather to tell the headquarters more about what is happening in operating units. The objectives that come up to the Secretary's office and OMB tend to be safe objectives, that is, they propose doing things already known to the men on top and to take such steps as those in the line can feel most confident that they can deliver. In this way, managers can hope to avoid the conflict arising from considering controversial objectives.

The identification of a particular level of government official as a client for the MbO system is meaningful in organizational analysis, where the limits of inquiry are set by the boundaries of the organization. But in a broader perspective, the federal executive is only part of a political system with ramifications throughout society. From such a viewpoint, the government may be seen as a producer of programs intended to achieve objectives that are consumed by citizens in society. It is important to consider to what extent the beneficiaries of the MbO system are officials within government, or citizens in society. Insofar as objectives refer to internal operations of government, and agencies are themselves the principal beneficiaries, then MbO, like many management techniques, is only of interest to students of what goes on inside organizations. Insofar as objectives refer to changes in the world out there, beyond the corridors of the federal agencies, then the system is of wider political interest.

The beneficiaries of any organization, including government, can be broadly grouped under two headings: reflexive and transitive. (Mohr, 1973: 475ff) Where goals are *transitive*, then the beneficiaries will belong to the world outside government. Where goals are *reflexive*, they provide benefits for those inside government. To describe the activities of government in terms of helping people is to see government in terms of transitive goals. To describe the chief concern of public officials as helping themselves, that is, expending resources to maintain bureaucratic morale, is to posit reflexive goals. Any large organization such as the United States government must have *both* transitive and reflexive goals. A government must manage its institutions and sustain the morale of its own employees, otherwise it will collapse. Yet a government must also be concerned with delivering goods and services to groups of its citizens, or it will be isolated from the society around it.

The first concern of public officials is to get a handle on a problem, that is, find some means by which they can come to grips with it. This is a precondition of effective management, seen in hands-on terms. If a department defines problems as caused by its own deficiencies, reflexive objectives are appropriate. Or it can define problems as caused by an identifiable organization out there, e.g., a chemical works that issues pollutants, or landlords that maintain slum houses. In each instance, it can act through legal powers, with one formal organization, government, dealing with another formal organization, e.g., a chemical company or a property company. If the problem is defined in terms of the natural and physical environment, then the government seeks to make an impact upon relatively inert natural objects, e.g., a hillside awaiting a bulldozer. Engineering technology, rather than social and economic considerations, becomes of first importance. When the object of action is a complex social or economic process, then there is no handle for program managers to grab.

The difficulties in managing federal programs directed at poor people, a poorly organized and often unstable category, have led the government to shift emphasis to the provision of funds to state and local governments that may find it easier to manage a problem closer to them. In efforts to reduce black unemployment, the Johnson Administration concentrated upon pumping money and services into urban ghettos, in the belief that influencing the social system of blacks would lead them to steadier, better jobs. When this did not happen as quickly as expected, the Nixon Administration switched emphasis. Instead of trying to influence a social process, it sought to influence corporations on which it could get a handle. It strengthened clauses concerning minority employment practices in contracts with federal defense contractors, and with universities in receipt of federal grants. Moreover, it hired compliance officers to hold private organizations accountable for what the government's own programs had been unable to achieve, namely, increase minority employment.

The statements generated in the MbO system provide an unusually comprehensive assortment of materials about the intended beneficiaries of government activities, because of the range of departments participating and the emphasis upon activities leading to observable consequences within a relatively short period of time. Many MbO statements contain explicit references in their descriptions of goals, identifying the final consumer of their results. In other instances, the author has been able to identify consumers (that is, the principal parties likely to be affected) from the context of departmental justifications or related statements. Table 8.1 shows who or what will be most directly affected by the achievement of 1974 and 1975 Presidential objectives. The pattern is much the same in both years. In about two-thirds of all instances, government actions are transitive, that is, someone (or something) out there is meant to benefit, however complex the sequence of inputs and outputs. The recipients of government benefits are heterogeneous; some are not aimed at helping people, but rather at juristic persons, i.e., corporations, or at making an impact upon the natural environment. The slight fluctuations between the two years arise from the inclusion of the State Department, with its external orientation in year two, and the omission of Defense objectives, substantially concerned with management within the department.

A comparison of the groups immediately affected by the achievement of Presidential objectives and ultimate consumers of particular fiscal year objectives shows that the apparent concentration upon within-government concerns arises only because these are necessary means to further ends. For example, HEW will have to review and evaluate a problem or secure passage of legislation, before its actions can affect groups in society. Comparison of the forms of fiscal year objectives with the consumers of second-order benefits in the longer term (Tables 6.2 and Table 8.1) shows that the proportion directed outside government doubles. Overall, about one-third of objectives directly relate to the world outside government, one-third relate to the world outside through a lengthy chain of causation, and about one-third feed back into government itself as the ultimate consumer.

Groups of Americans are the identifiable beneficiaries of 20 per cent of 1974 MbO statements, and 18 per cent of those in the second year. Departments traditionally concerned with individual welfare, such as HEW, Labor and the Veterans Administration, contribute a disproportionate number of these objectives. Defense registered six social objectives in 1974, because the politically aware Pentagon is concerned with the social welfare of those dependent upon it. For example, drug addiction in the armed forces, minority employment, and the social consequences of closing defense installations in one-industry communities. The Department of Agriculture is concerned with farmers as people, as well as with farmers as productive units in the economy, stating four social objectives. In all, fifteen agencies in 1974 and thirteen the following year reported objectives intended to benefit groups of Americans. In addition, 5 per cent of objectives in 1974 and 6 per cent in 1975 were intended to improve the social

TABLE 8.1.  The Consumers of Government Actions

|  | 1974 % | 1974 N | 1975 % | 1975 N |
|---|---|---|---|---|
| **A.  *Outside Consumers*** | | | | |
| Members of American Society | | | | |
| Categories of persons | 25% | 20   47 | 24% | 18   41 |
| Social processes, relationships | | 5   13 | | 6   14 |
| The Economy | | | | |
| Corporations | 22% | 10   23 | 24% | 10   23 |
| Economic processes, relationships | | 12   29 | | 14   32 |
| Physical and Natural Environment | | 12   29 | | 8   18 |
| International System, Processes | | 5   13 | | 13   29 |
| Subtotal | | 64 | | 69 |
| **B.  *Inside Consumers*** | | | | |
| Institutions of Government | | | | |
| The department initiating action | | 20   47 | | 15   33 |
| Other executive departments | | 6   15 | | 6   14 |
| State and local government | | 9   21 | | 9   21 |
| Subtotal | | 35 | | 30 |

system, e.g., to develop "a safe and efficient national system for blood collection, distribution and utilization." Benefits provided the social system do not have easily identified recipients, as do categoric welfare programs with explicit qualifications for individual entitlement. But they can be pervasive in significance, because they are inputs to the social system of relationships, and are not confined to target categories of individuals.

The bulk of the 22 per cent of the 1974 objectives concerned with the economy and the 24 per cent in 1975 were intended to improve the economic system as a whole, rather than being targeted at specific corporations or industries. The two main economic departments—Treasury and Commerce—are primarily concerned with objectives that disperse benefits broadly, e.g., reforming the international monetary system, or increasing exports. Interior and the Environmental Protection Agency are noteworthy in that many of their objectives, while intended to benefit society eventually, are specifically targeted at corporations whose actions change the environment, e.g., through mineral exploitation, strip mining, laying pipe lines, or the emitting of pollutants.

The physical and natural environment is the intended final recipient of the impact of 12 per cent of 1974 objectives and 8 per cent the following year. The agencies chiefly responsible for this cluster of objectives—Interior, the Environmental Protection Agency and the Atomic Energy Commission—together account for three-quarters of them. The beneficiaries are here mineral or vegetable, rather than animal and social. In such cases social concerns are incidental rather than ends in themselves. The differing perspectives can be harmonized, e.g., social conservation helps farmers as well as the soil, and nature conservation provides recreation areas as well as protecting the natural environment. But the energy crisis has shown that different ideas of who or what is to benefit from environmental policies can lead to conflicting policy prescriptions.

The number of objectives concerned with the international system in 1974 (5 per cent) rose in the second year to 13 per cent because of the participation of the State Department. It could be argued that America's international objectives are intended to benefit Americans collectively, and, in the case of international economic concerns, to bring benefits to firms or groups of Americans. But in causal terms it is better to see American foreign policy actions as inputs to a system dispersing benefits to many countries. The cooperative game nature of international relations mean that objectives can be achieved only when the interests of several countries are met.

A maximum of 30 to 35 per cent of objectives in the two years considered here are reflexive, if the whole of government is treated as a single unit. But if only those statements are considered reflexive in which the department initiating action is also the final beneficiary, then the proportion drops to 15 to 20 per cent. In the remainder of cases, another federal agency, or state and local institutions are the final consumer of its actions. From the perspective of a single agency, another federal department, the White House, state office buildings, and city halls belong to a world out there. They can be as difficult to influence as a recalcitrant business firm or an elusive category of poor people.

A case by case examination of reflexive objectives shows that individually they are readily justified as positive contributions to the ongoing work of government. They do not reflect a bureaucratic desire to empire build; instead they show the overhead costs of doing business as a government. In two departments, a strong emphasis upon reflexive objectives shows a justifiable desire to improve management and/or respect for the institutions of federalism. The Justice Department registered seven reflexive statements, mixing management concerns, e.g., "to improve its management direction and program effectiveness," and objectives concerned with coordinating law enforcement work, e.g., the reporting of criminal statistics. In 1974 HUD registered fifteen reflexive statements, registering in almost equal parts the very big internal review of management and policy that it was conducting and its statutory obligations to work through state and local government.

The difficulty in determining whether the distribution of beneficiaries is a good mixture is explained by Miles' law: "Where you stand depends upon where you sit." Viewed from the perspective of a social worker or a sociologist, more than three-quarters of the objectives analyzed in Table 8.1 might be said to be off target, because they do not have groups of individuals or social relationships as their final point of impact. From the viewpoint of an economist, more than three-quarters of objectives appear either irrelevant or subordinate to the government's essential role of managing the economy. A specialist in military affairs might argue that the sine qua non of government—defending the nation in a perilous international system—is even more neglected. Each of these statements tells us more about the priorities of the speaker than it does about the priorities of government. Government actions, insofar as they are reflected in the MbO system, provide some things for different kinds of beneficiaries.

Proponents of management by objectives (and of many other techniques for better management in government) view the policy process, as depicted in Figure 6.1, by reading from left to right, that is, looking first at what one must do immediately and whether (as well as how many) milestones have been passed. By contrast, the citizen is likely to read the process from right to left. He will look first of all at conditions within society, and work backwards to demand some signs of government action, if the impact of established programs appears unsatisfactory. The contrast in perspective reflects the difference between viewing political objectives from the producer's role, as a Presidential appointee or public official, or from the consumer's role as citizen.

In a federal system of government, with legislative and executive powers separated, pushing things through can be an arduous and time-consuming task, taking anything from two to ten years from the identification of a problem to the passage and implementation of laws benefitting intended consumers. One reason for the introduction of MbO was the belief that too often the White House as well as Congress exhausted its interest in the policy process by the enactment of a bill *before* its benefits could begin to be brought to intended consumers. The leaders of management reform at OMB believe that the effective delivery of promised policies is just as important, if not more important, than starting more programs. MbO was meant, inter alia, to monitor the efficiency and effectiveness with which government programs are delivered to citizens.

The political model of management by objectives is producer oriented; it concentrates attention upon what can be *pushed through* the political system. It starts from the supply side, as is fitting for persons who produce government policies. The objectives of government are identified by political leaders and bureaucratic officials who advise them. Once these are settled, then the MbO system is intended to monitor and motivate public officials to carry out agreed programs. Good government is that which most efficiently and effectively pushes through the actions required to reach its (that is, the producers') objectives. The model is most appropriate for reflexive objectives, especially those in which the federal government is itself both producer and consumer of a program. In activities involving the transformation of physical and national resources, the government must push through to its objectives, because the final recipients of its actions remain inert.

Among citizens voicing demands for government action, the model best describing their view of politics is one that emphasizes how they can *pull out* what they want from government. Potential consumers of benefits are immediately concerned with the speed with which government passes milestones and achieves objectives and goals, because they are waiting, with their hands out, or with their hands reaching into institutions, to pull out benefits of immediate concern to themselves. For example, students entitled to cash payments under the GI Bill are likely to monitor more closely the efficiency with which the Veterans Administration sends out checks than will any VA official.

The ordinary citizen is consumer oriented, rather than producer oriented. Government actions should be demand driven, responding to his wishes, rather than producer driven. Moreover, in a liberal as opposed to a totalitarian society, the ordinary citizen expects to satisfy many of his demands reflexively, that is, by looking after himself. When the ordinary citizen turns to government, he is primarily concerned with what he can pull out from it. He will monitor the performance of government most closely when he is waiting for benefits. The frustrations that a citizen experiences when an anticipated benefit is delayed or denied are likely to be more important that preferences or wants temporarily stimulated during an electoral campaign. The civil rights and welfare rights movements of the 1960s demonstrated that even people with low income and low status can be organized effectively to pull out benefits from government. Up to 30 per cent of outside objectives could be monitored by consumer groups, for there are organized or organizable consumers—whether AFDC mothers, or companies seeking outer continental shelf oil leases—who will take out some benefit if a government objective is achieved. (Table 8.1)

When the objective is to modify a social or economic system, actions cannot be monitored by potential consumers, because there is no organized group at hand to pull things out from government, nor can government contract with a formal organization to deliver the goods. Nor can government be sure of achieving its goal by pushing through milestones, for there are no handles to grasp in system processes; the outputs of systems of relationships are uncertain and uncontrolled by any single organization. The most appropriate model to describe government activity in this situation is that of *pumping out* goods and services, hoping that its output will change the system in the direction it wishes. For example, the balanced international investment pattern that the Treasury identifies as an MbO objective is the joint product (or the by-product) of hundreds or thousands of decisions taken by foreign as well as American public and private organizations in a continuing, and not necessarily stable, process of partisan mutual adjustment.

In a fourth model of government, public officials are *shaking hands with themselves* when they are both the producers and consumers of objectives. When the ultimate beneficiary of an objective, for example, an improved accounting system, is within the department initiating the action, those trying to push through activities can be guided by colleagues trying to pull out benefits from the program.

There remain conflicts within departments as well as between the department and the world outside, including other parts of government. But these are likely to be less than those between the department and the world outside.

The models summarize four different ways of giving direction to those with hands-on control of the actions of government. When government is pushing through a program, then the hands that count are those of officials within government. When clients are pulling out what they want, the hands that count are those of citizens, or their elected representatives in Congress. When government is pumping goods into a complex and imperfectly understood system lacking controlling handles, it is handing off its responsibilities. When government officials are only shaking hands with each other, the resulting sense of self-congratulation may be good for bureaucratic morale, but it is of little immediate public benefit.

American political values emphasize the importance of the citizen as sovereign, whether as political animal or as a consumer in the market place. Moreover, the emphasis upon citizen involvement in government has grown in the past decade. This suggests that the most important questions of politics will best be monitored when consumers can see how well the government is making progress in meeting their demands. To improve the way in which the government goes about achieving its most important political objectives, measures should be taken to increase the voice of consumers and potential consumers, whether organized or not. Conceivably, the issuance of "impact statements" might stimulate potential beneficiaries (and losers) to organize to pull out or push back the delivery of programs distributing benefits and costs unevenly throughout society.

If public officials find that there is no way to turn a problem into something manageable along lines suggested above, then they may pump out goods and services, in hopes that the social theories explicit or implicit in their programs will lead to desired benefits. In circumstances of uncertainty, when there is an imperfect understanding about what is required, public officials run the risk of pursuing activities that are milestones on the road to nowhere.

# 9

# The Limitations
# of Technique

*Organization cannot make a genius out of an incompetent; even less can it, of itself, make the decisions which are required to trigger necessary action. On the other hand, disorganization can scarcely fail to result in inefficiency and can easily lead to disaster.*

Dwight D. Eisenhower

*A year is a very short time to change the behavior of the bureaucracy.*

Anonymous Department of Labor official

Just as some problems do not have an answer, so too answers can be devised for which there is no appropriate problem. Management associates have demonstrated, sceptics notwithstanding, that an MbO system can be put into operation within the federal government. But the thought then arises: given that it works, to what problem is it an answer? The absence of White House involvement and the limited impact of the system within the Office of Management and Budget shows that management by objectives is not related to the chief concerns of the central institutions of the executive branch. Yet to say that it will not resolve central problems of government direction does not prove that it is not useful within limits.

The experience in applying MbO since 1973 provides a fair assessment of the value of the technique. The political backing given to management by objectives by the President and the Director and Deputy Director of OMB represents the maximum central support that a management system might attain. And the commitment of all three men to better management of existing government programs, as well as (or instead of) the creation of new programs, represents an unusually high degree of concern by top-level leaders with the management of the executive branch. There has also been a signifi-

131

cant commitment of competent personnel—both at OMB and agency level—to give the MbO system the opportunity to work. Management staff have had substantial incentives to do so, because their own career evaluation is immediately affected by what they do. The political and manpower resources are thus a generously endowed test of MbO in government. Moreover, it was introduced at a time when Democrats, Republicans, and nonparty commentators agreed that there *is* a problem of managing the work of government.

Notwithstanding variations from department to department, the MbO system displays a number of common features in its application throughout the federal executive. The most important political characteristics are the following:

1. The MbO system does not introduce new concepts to the management of government work. Attention to objectives, progress chasing and a list of things to do are timeless qualities of good management. What the MbO system provides is a new emphasis upon themes that were obscured in the concentration upon choice and legislation in the go-go days of the Great Society. Moreover, it offers a technique for *systematically* and *periodically* reviewing progress toward objectives, in a way that invests ongoing management activities with more significance, through the participation of Presidential appointees and staff from the Executive Office of the President.

2. The MbO system concentrates upon operating activities within the department, and not upon questions of political choice. The distinction is made evident by the large proportion of objectives committing a department to evaluate and report recommendations about what should be done in a potentially controversial problem area. The MbO statement normally does not prescribe what the recommendation should or should not include. Political, i.e., controversial guidelines are omitted. Instead, the emphasis is upon the seemingly simple requirement that something be recommended by the stated deadline. The system works better as a means of prodding a departmental committee than as a device for forcing the Secretary, OMB, or the White House to take a decision about the recommendations brought forward. The latter type of recommendation is part of the politics of choice, an area that MbO staff do not enter.

3. The crucial activities involving the MbO system occur within departments. MbO statements are concerned with operating activities of specific units in particular departments; they are not concerned with functions that are the responsibility of everybody, and therefore of nobody, e.g., "the efficient expenditure of public money," nor are they concerned with anything as general and multidepartmental as "providing for the needs of low income families." The statements are always related to a specific organizational unit, be-

cause this is the place where, if at all, things can get done. The role of OMB and the Office of the Secretary or the Under-Secretary is to review action, to stimulate action when progress lags, and to facilitate or redirect action when this is necessary.

The MbO system is a part of the management process, not a discrete activity that can be assigned to a staff to carry out on its own. Within a departmental context, the prime responsibility for meeting MbO objectives rests with line managers. Insofar as these objectives simply register what bureau chiefs would be concerned about in any event, the system does not require additional work on their part—except for filling out forms that are, by bureaucratic standards, relatively simple paper games. The system requires only that line managers achieve what they said they would achieve in the course of their regular activities. The staff assigned to work full time on the MbO system in a department are few, of middle rank in the bureaucracy, and maintain a low profile, usually within the office of an Assistant Secretary for Administration and Management. They have neither the political weight nor the formal authority to give directions as and when they believe an operating unit is not making satisfactory progress toward an agreed objective. The most the staff can do is to refer the problem upwards. The separation of oversight from management responsibilities is normal in the federal government. The MbO system is politically weak because, in the first instance at least, its full-time staff do not control resources upon which line managers depend, as do budget examiners exercising financial oversight for the same programs.

To assess the benefits of management by objectives requires a standard for judgment. What are the objectives of management by objectives? The initial 1973 memorandum sent out by the Director of OMB to department heads listed six main goals for the program. These rather diffusely worded statements can be grouped under three broad headings: (1) improved communication, (2) faster problem spotting, and (3) improved accountability of managers to supervisors.

1. The *communications* objectives of the MbO program were stated in terms that do not permit easy assessment:

a.  Establish an environment for better decision making by having an ongoing year-round process for top-level agency and executive office discussions and interaction.
b.  Establish a mutual understanding between departments and the executive office of what the major administration objectives are in each department.
c.  Provide better information to counsellors and others to identify priorities and coordinate efforts.

The management conferences between departments and OMB provide a periodic occasion for discussing agency activities with OMB. Even after allowing for the tendency of OMB officials to cancel meetings, the system has probably increased the number of discussions between OMB directors and department heads about the management of substantive programs because there were nearly none before. The annual statement of Presidential objectives provides a more stable agenda of program concerns than fire-fighting pressures produce. It thus increases communication about matters that otherwise tend to be neglected, because of events viewed as more important politically within the Executive Office and the Office of the Secretary. Moreover, the MbO system concentrates attention upon the same concerns for a year or more. Given the high turnover of Presidential appointees in departments there is some value in institutionalizing an agenda of shared concerns. The agenda for communication is not about decision making, but rather a review of decision achievement.

The second and third points emphasize the direction of communication between the Executive Office and departments. Departments are meant to receive (and attend to) more direction from Executive Office spokesmen about major administration objectives, whether Presidential counsellors or undefined "others." The White House was in no position to assert direction for most of the period considered here, because the trauma of Watergate broke almost concurrently with the introduction of MbO. One can therefore only speculate how John Ehrlichman or Robert Haldeman might have tried to use the MbO system had they remained in their posts.

The MbO system cannot prevent a department from giving a high priority to an objective that is of little White House interest. OMB can and does occasionally remove objectives from departmental submissions as beneath Presidential notice. The excluded objectives need not be abandoned. A department can simply classify it as a departmental objective, and monitor progress independently of OMB. The MbO system can be used to make departments add objectives to which they would not otherwise give priority. The MbO system does not create influence where none exists, but rather provides another opportunity for senior OMB officials, White House staff, and even the President to bring such influence as they have to bear upon departments. The provisions for monitoring progress toward Presidential objectives mean that any top down additions to the list should not be lost sight of by the department, or, for that matter, by the person who launched the suggestion. The restricted political importance of MbO statements, however, offers little incentive for White House staff to use the mechanism to press priorities upon departments. This can be done more quickly through direct contact. Moreover, there is a risk in the White House or OMB forcing a department to add a priority: the department may later use this as an argument why it should be given greater top-level backing to achieve the aim.

2. The routine monitoring of agreed actions is valuable in the exceptional case when it spots problems early enough to permit resolution. The problems are not major political concerns of the country, such as poor housing, regional unemployment, or clusters of poverty. These are monitored through conventional means of voicing political grievances. The problems spotted in MbO are specific to the executive branch, the management problems of getting things done. The failure of government to do what it announces it will do is embarrassing, and, cumulatively, presents political problems. The MbO system asks: What difficulties have program managers unearthed in carrying out their assigned tasks? The MbO reporting mechanism encourages managers to report awkward news before it has festered into really bad news. The management conference agenda gives an opportunity to program managers to bring up unanticipated difficulties that they might otherwise hesitate to bring to the attention of their superiors. Because they know they are being monitored, program managers have an incentive to report difficulties promptly, rather than suppress them and risk having events later bring them to the attention of their superiors in a hotter and bigger form. In short, MbO encourages fire prevention or fighting fires while they are small, before they get out of hand and blaze in full public view.

3. In the business world, *accountability* is an important feature of a management-by-objectives system. High-level decision makers and line managers are expected to agree between them what is expected of the manager of each program; the statement of annual objectives becomes a contract, complete with clauses offering rewards for success and penalties for failure. OMB gave prominence to two objectives concerning accountability:

a.  Identify who is responsible for a particular objective, what requirements are necessary to meet the objectives, and assure Executive Office support where appropriate.
b.  Provide an improved method for evaluating overall departmental performance and the performance of key individuals.

Fixing responsibility upon individuals is extremely difficult in government. There are uncertainties about the level in the hierarchy at which to fix responsibility. The President can make a Cabinet Secretary answer for his department's achievement of Presidential objectives. To do this does not, however, identify the person who will do the work, but only a scapegoat who can be blamed if things go wrong. As one descends the organization hierarchy, responsibilities for actions often are divided out among several units within a department, thus blurring responsibility. The MbO system focusses responsibility by concentrating upon objectives that can be assigned to specific units within a department. Broad aspirations that cut across many units within a department can either be left out, on·the ground that everyone knows what the department's mission is, or else cast in the form of long-term goals, e.g., energy conservation or fighting inflation, about which everyone in the government is concerned, but for which no one in particular is accountable.

The MbO system has undoubtedly provided management associates in OMB with substantial evidence "for evaluating overall departmental performance." Evaluation began when management associates noted that some departments are better than others at stating what their objectives are. The preparations for OMB-departmental management conferences give management associates both informal and formal opportunities to evaluate the work of departments that they monitor. Knowledge—or at least, a shrewd suspicion —of what is going wrong and who is the cause of it is insufficient to make a program manager accountable, either to OMB or even to his own Secretary. This will occur only if those to whom reports are made have rewards and sanctions related to the performance of key individuals. This is not the case. The rewards that can be offered political appointees or civil servants are few, beyond such intangibles as Secretarial favor or peer group recognition. MbO staff speak more often of sanctions to prod laggards than of rewards. Some sanctions are weak, e.g., "No one likes to stand up before his peers and the Secretary and make excuses for failures or mistakes," or even frequent out-of-town travel intended to make the official resign. Short of a radical transformation of established civil service procedures, e.g., something analogous to medieval tax farming or the award of knighthoods to civil servants as in Britain, there are severe limits to a payment by results approach to program management.

The chief achievements of the management-by-objectives system are matters of degree. The system has not changed the management of government in kind—nor did anyone expect this except a few enthusiasts in the initial flush of taking on a new job. The MbO system has encouraged, to a limited and unmeasurable extent, more communication about continuing programs between OMB and the departments, and within departments where the system is supported by Presidential appointees. It has occasionally spotted problems before they become fires big enough to be seen from the heights of OMB. It has given officials in OMB and the departmental office of the Secretary better insight into problems and achievements in program management, but it has not greatly altered their ability to reward or punish those accountable for what gets done in the name of government. The influence of MbO, such as it is, has been consistent with consensual goals of good management. Few would advocate that the federal government should avoid communication within the executive branch, allow problems to pile up until explosions occur, or launch programs without any interest in whether those in charge are keeping them to schedule.

The costs of the MbO system are more easily identified, because they are expressed in terms of money and manpower. The notional money cost of the MbO system is trivial, in terms of the federal budget, but significant within OMB's own budget. The approximate costs of running the system within OMB might be assessed at about $1.5 million of OMB's 1974 budget, since the MbO staff constitutes about 7.5 per cent of the agency's professional personnel. The cost of operating the system in the departments is twice or three times the OMB operations, because the bulk of the work must be done within departments. On such a basis, the MbO system costs from $4.5 million to $6 million a year to operate. Spending more money on the MbO system would not produce more or better results. The difficulties of strengthening MbO are structural rather than financial. For example, reform of the civil service would be required to overcome the problems arising in fixing accountability and assessing rewards in relation to the achievement of objectives.

The actual cost of running the MbO system is less than the bookkeeping cost of management staff, because a substantial proportion of staff time is not spent on MbO work. This is particularly true of OMB itself, where half or more of management associates' time is spent on fire-fighting activities, or upon special analytic studies that arise initially from discussing objectives with departments. In terms of the scarce time of the Director and Deputy Director, the cost has been limited by an unwillingness to invest as much time as originally budgeted in management conferences with department heads. Moreover, there has been no tendency for the costs of the MbO system to escalate, for those in charge are firm in wishing to avoid the creation of a paper-chasing activity. Since objectives can only be achieved by managers, there is a low ceiling upon the number of management staff reckoned necessary to monitor progress. The greatest need for staff has been in the initial period of establishing MbO in the agencies.

The most effective way to strengthen the MbO system, in theory at least, would be to link it with the budget process. The very name of the Office of Management and Budget calls attention to the interrelationship between financial resources and managing to get things done. In their most optimistic moments, Roy Ash and Fred Malek believed that they could concentrate attention upon government objectives *per se*, making debates about money secondary to questions of ends. This would benefit political heads of departments reviewing requests from bureau chiefs, as well as OMB, reviewing departmental requests on behalf of the President. Immediately, it would provide OMB with a list of objectives that could be monitored once budget requests were approved, and enable it to use its institutional memory to compare this year's departmental achievements with last year's appropriation, as well as with objectives for the next year. By making departments more conscious of how they spent what they got, as well as how they justified what they wanted, management effectiveness and efficiency might be improved. Not least, linking MbO objectives to the budget would give the system status, by making it part of the central link between OMB and the agencies, and promise permanent institutionalization as a routine part of the budget submission and review.

MbO staff have been divided about the value of forging links between their statements of objectives and the budget process. *If* the MbO system could make both department staff and budget examiners concentrate upon political objectives first and look at their costs secondarily, then it would fundamentally change the way that Presidential priorities are indicated to departments. On the other hand, for MbO staff to claim greater prominence for their statements in the crucial decisions of budget review would risk failure and the rapid demise of MbO, or relegation to an attic where previous management innovations are stored within OMB.

The attempt to link management by objectives with budgeting was made in 1974, in the process of budgeting for fiscal year 1976. When OMB issued its A-11 form to departments in June, 1974, stipulating procedures to be followed in filing requests for money for the forthcoming fiscal year of 1976, agencies were asked to include a statement of their chief departmental objectives and "specifically to discuss them in the context of the agency written justification material." Agencies were also asked to include preliminary statements of milestones marking progress toward these objectives and indications of the "end results that will be produced" and wherever applicable, to provide some kind of performance measures. In a sense, the change was simply intended to make explicit what has always been implicit, or else inferential, in budget statements: that money allotted will be spent for a purpose. If it is obvious what these purposes are, then requesting MbO statements would cost little effort, and provide little advantage. Insofar as departmental statements are either non-obvious or obviously not acceptable, then there could be gains in knowledge (and, potentially, in better decision making) by requiring explicit statements.

The timing of the OMB circular recognized that, initially at least, the choice of objectives could not determine budget priorities, but rather that objectives would be added on to departmental requests after budget priorities had been shaped. This happened because agencies were already working on their budget requests for Fiscal Year 1976 (for which Presidential recommendations were due in January, 1975) *before* receipt of the A-11 circular of June 28, 1974. Moreover, they had not yet had their statement of 1975 objectives approved by OMB or the President.

Requiring MbO statements in the budget submission is not a guarantee that the statements will be of any significance, as is shown by the history of efforts to introduce PPBS into the budget process. In the words of one OMB official, "Bureaucrats will write down anything you ask if they think it will help them get money." Nor are the objectives that a department offers OMB binding upon its subsequent actions, as are objectives that Congress may mandate upon a department in the course of writing appropriations bills.

The incorporation of MbO statements in the budget process failed, because the Directors of OMB did not themselves wish to make use of the materials requested and provided. Top-down concern with MbO was vitiated by two factors. The first was the declining importance of the budget review process to the Director, because of the increasing amount of time he spends in the White House in his role as Presidential counsellor, an activity outside the program-by-program, agency-by-agency routine of budget review. In 1974 Roy Ash was a lame-duck Director, and Fred Malek had already resigned as Deputy Director. Secondly, no penalties fell on departments that did not perform well in terms of putting on paper statements of objectives. During the Fall, 1974 budget review hearings, departments that could make a clear statement of objectives in submitting claims, especially for additional funds, were at an advantage. But this arose, not from their use of MbO procedures, but rather from adopting a general analytical orientation compatible with that of OMB staff themselves. In effect, the MbO statements requested by OMB were like inserts in a looseleaf notebook, easily skipped or dispensed with. The budget review tested the influence of MbO in defining choices between objectives—and it was found wanting.

Ironically, the limits upon the use of management by objectives arise from characteristics of the sponsors of the system, the Office of Management and Budget. The Director and Deputy Director have made clear that they can only spend a limited amount of time with department heads, discussing the type of objectives registered by the system. They have also made clear that the system is not integral to the chief activity linking OMB to the departments, the budget review. Moreover, management associates within OMB have shown that they will invest only a limited amount of their working time in developing and maintaining the system, preferring to go where the action is fighting fires, or else go where the big bang is in special analytic studies about the future of programs costing hundreds of millions or billions of dollars annually.

Senior OMB officials recognize that the problems to which management by objectives are addressed remain real and important within the federal executive. From the top of OMB down (at least until one reaches the ranks of long-service budget examiners) there is a desire to concentrate attention upon evaluating the results of programs to complement the traditional budget examiner's concern with program costs. It is recognized that a program is not completed when all the money is spent, and a batch of valid receipts are in hand. It is only completed when objectives and goals are realized. The milestone measures that figure prominently in MbO usually carry a department only part of the way toward its goals or ideals. Senior OMB officials continue to seek a technique that will help them evaluate the ongoing activities of government so that the work of government can be better done.

The only way in which management by objectives can become more effective within the federal executive is by reducing its present intimate connection with OMB, and incorporating it in greater depth within the operating agencies of government. The first reason for this is that MbO is concerned with getting things done: hands-on control of what government does lies within the departments, and not in the Executive Office of the President. The second reason is equally important; departments will only be anxious to make a system work effectively insofar as it is seen as part of the department's own management process, and not something planted upon it to provide information or influence to OMB.

Yet to make the management-by-objectives system effective within a government department is a different thing from making it effective within OMB. Anything that the White House does in one department affects only a small proportion of executive branch activity. As one department may become better managed, another may be going downhill, in the face of novel problems or leadership by Presidential appointees with no interest in how their department manages to get things done. The White House can affect the direction of a government department by appointing political leaders. OMB can offer advice on various management problems from within its own staff—whether this is a part-time function of examiners with influence, or the first concern of much less influential management personnel. If this does not produce the results that the White House would like, then White House staff who placed the wrong men in charge may try to undercut their own appointees. Such a strategy is only likely to reduce the effectiveness of Presidential appointees further, without necessarily improving the effectiveness of those with "hands-on" control in operating units. The recurring failures of management improvement schemes introduced by OMB through the years argue that the limitations of the MbO system are not specific to the system, but rather arise from the difficulty of making *any* improvement to the management of the federal executive that would be significant in terms of the major political concerns of those who work in Washington.

The most important questions in American government (or in any government) will be monitored by a *political* process, that is, a process explicitly recognizing and providing for disputes about what government ought to be doing, as well as what it is doing. Because the management by objectives system is not concerned with choices between alternatives, it is, in effect, outside this political process, and thus, outside the immediate concern of political leaders, whether in the White House or in Congress. The limits of the technique cannot be overcome by altering the MbO system. Within its limited range of concerns, it does add a small but noteworthy voice to government. There is no need to transform it into a system of greater scope, embracing the identification of alternative programs, the choice between them, and planning their implementation. Such a system (PPBS) has already been invented—and it has already failed.

Management by objectives is best invoked for nonpolitical (i.e., noncontroversial) concerns of government. Where consumers are in agreement about what government should do, there are no political controversies to complicate the task of public officials. With consensus about objectives, officials can concentrate exclusively upon technical problems of how to get there from here, safe from the risk of being derailed en route or subject to a hail of brickbats when their objectives become known.

The proposition can be tested by examining the 1974 objectives to see to what extent they are political, that is, generate public controversy about their desirability. While every action of government can be described as controversial if there is less than 100 per cent approval, the costs of making controversy public are sufficient so that all private disagreements are not turned into public controversy. Government actions pass a critical threshold between being apolitical and political when opposition is sufficient to make a matter controversial in the press, in Congress, and within the executive branch. Initially, this analysis was intended to differentiate two types of controversy: disputes along nonpartisan lines, and disputes in which the participants are readily aligned along party lines. The distinction cannot be employed. The difficulty of classification does not arise from vagueness of objectives, but rather from uncertainty about the positions of the parties. Rather than invite disputes about what the parties really stand for, it is best to group together objectives that invite controversy whatever the reason.

Of the Presidential objectives, 81 per cent were apolitical in 1974 and 80 per cent in 1975; only one-fifth involved political controversy. The apolitical objectives are of four main types. Some avoided controversy because they referred to consensual aims, e.g., the encouragement of effective cancer research. Others did so because they pledged the preparation of a departmental report or program about a current issue, but avoided giving any specific direction influencing the report. For example, while there are disagreements about what, if anything, the federal government should do about a national health service, there can be no disagreement with the principle that HEW should "develop and submit to Congress the Administration's proposal for National Health Insurance." The job of a department is to respond to demands for action, just as the concern of those getting Presidential objectives is that the objective should not constitute a commitment to a particular recommendation. A third type of noncontroversial objective involves the implementation of an Act of Congress or other valid directive. While the law may have been the subject of controversy when debated on the Hill, Congressmen cannot dispute that federal agencies should try to implement what a majority of Congress has approved. A fourth type of objective is noncontroversial because it involves actions that are unlikely to be opposed by politically active groups. For example, an objective about giving financial assistance to small business cannot be challenged by big business, without inviting questions about benefits given them, nor can it be challenged by the average taxpayer, because his personal interest is insufficient to mobilize opposition.

MbO objectives are politically controversial for any combination of four reasons. If an objective seeks to promote legislation, it is reasonable to suppose that there will be some opposition to it in Congress. An objective that adversely affects identifiable states or Congressional districts (e.g., the closure of military bases) will invite opposition from representatives of these areas without regard to party. Similarly, objectives that adversely affect organized interest groups (e.g., changes in maritime subsidies) will stimulate opposition in Congress. A handful of objectives that concerned the reorganization or dismantling of Great Society programs could stimulate controversy along party lines, insofar as liberal Democrats continued to identify with major programs of the Johnson Administration, and Republicans opposed them.

Cabinet departments are much readier to get involved in political controversy than non-Cabinet agencies. Five-sixths of all the controversial MbO objectives came from Cabinet departments in each year. In the case of Interior and Treasury, involvement in controversy follows from the prominence given legislation in their schedule of Presidential objectives. In the case of HEW and HUD, it results from the Republican Administration's selective rejection of parts of its legacy from the Johnson Administration. Among the non-Cabinet agencies, only the Environmental Protection Agency has often been involved in controversial objectives. This has occurred because it is charged with making progress in an area where support is strong enough to create an EPA, but not strong enough to eliminate opposition from interest groups adversely affected by antipollution measures. The lesser status of most non-Cabinet agencies in part reflects that much of their work is nonpolitical. The potential for public controversy in such service agencies as GSA or the Civil Service Commission is slight, and there is less in such action agencies as the Veterans Administration or the Small Business Administration than in Agriculture, HEW, or Justice.

Management-by-objectives statements are often so near and yet so far from controversy because they avoid commitment to any particular choice, while simultaneously committing a department to move in the direction of some choice. The President can endorse an HEW statement about formulating plans relating to a national health service, because it only commits him to accept the obvious: if Congress is to debate health legislation, then the executive branch should prepare a position too. The prechoice stage of the policy process involves a significant movement from non-decision making to actions where a positive choice is likely to be made. But it does not involve controversy at the moment it enters the MbO system.

The management-by-objectives system can handle government actions that fall between the purely routine, exciting neither interest nor controversy, and the strictly political, where controversy and interest are joined. Registration in the list of Presidential objectives can be the first stage that an issue reaches if a substantive problem has been identified without   government commitment to act: that is a review and report objective. Programs can appear in MbO statements when all that remains for the government to do is to implement an agreed compromise. Or an MbO objective may be a matter of interest to professionals responsible for a program within and outside government, but not reflect political differences. MbO objectives can certainly be important to those producing the actions, and to those affected by them, but they are of secondary significance in government, by comparison with controversial issues. The price that must be paid for the introduction of management techniques from outside the political process is that it is confined to those actions of government where politics is of least importance. A sizeable proportion of MbO staff assume this, because they prefer to think of themselves as apolitical managers, rather than as men concerned with giving controversial direction to government.

Political leaders must themselves monitor the uncertain progress of the controversial policies that occupy the center of concern in Washington at any given moment. They are likely to concentrate upon choices between program alternatives, given the low incentives for attending to program implementation, unless discretionary actions are intrinsically controversial or have been made controversial by political protest. Monitoring the most controversial stages of major policies will give political leaders the information and commitment that is needed to prepare them for major decisions that do lie within their power, e.g., deciding what legislation to recommend to the White House or Congress, or what compromises to accept there. But controversies are also monitored by Congress, the press and, not least, interest groups claiming to represent the views of affected consumers who know what they want to take out of government. In such circumstances, agreement about the government's objective is the *last* step in the political process, not the first. It is only *after* agreement has been reached that the MbO system can begin to come into effect.

# 10

# Does the President
# Have Objectives?

*No man ever saw a government. I live in the midst of the government of
the United States, but I never saw the government of the United States.*

Woodrow Wilson, 1916

*The federal government remains largely a collection of fragmented
bureau fiefdoms unable to co-ordinate with themselves intelligently.*

Heineman Task Force on Government Organization, 1967

The difficulty of identifying government objectives does not arise
from the absence of a sense of purpose in politics, but rather because
government is overflowing with objectives. The problem is deciding
*which* objectives are of most political significance, that is, controlling
when government actions become matters of controversy.

Any judgment about who decides government objectives depends
upon *where* objectives are thought to be determined. A producer's
model of government presupposes that objectives are determined by
the head(s) of an organization. But a consumer's model of governing
assumes that they are determined by voters who expect to benefit
from government actions. A study that starts by asking questions
about political objectives inevitably leads to questions about the
institutions of government itself.

The executive branch that the President heads is but a part of the
federal government; in turn, the federal government is but a part of
the multitiered institutions of American government. What is most
important here is that the executive branch itself is not an integrated
organization. Cronin (1974a: 472) aptly describes it as "a many

splintered thing." This fragmentation has profound and pervasive effects upon the role of the President, the one man who is concerned with the whole, rather than the parts, of the federal executive. Instead of being the head of a hierarchical body of officials who look up to him for authority, the President finds that both law and politics make him the titular head of institutions that lack corporeal unity. The federal executive is a label that describes a variety of entities lumped together; it does not refer to a single body politic. Analytically, the different departments and agencies of the executive branch have many things in common. But these common attributes—authorization by Act of Congress, regulation by rulings of the Supreme Court, dependence upon Congressional appropriations, and chiefs appointed by the President subject to Senate confirmation—are evidence of dependence upon authority outside the executive branch, as well as inside it.

While it is usually straightforward to say whether a government agency belongs to the executive branch, it is far more difficult to say *to whom* it belongs. The government that the President heads is characterized by independence of organizations within the executive branch, and interdependence across the institutional divisions of American federal government. The situation is not unique to government. Harlan Cleveland, (1972: 32) an administrator with experience of both government and large private sector organizations, describes contemporary organizations thus:

> *Growing size in turn is directly correlated with wider dispersion of real power inside each system, and also with more sharing of real responsibility with outsiders. In these circumstances the making of "decisions" cannot be described or understood in the recommendations up/orders down language of hierarchical administration. The devolution of responsibility goes mostly outward, not downward.*

The federal executive can perhaps best be characterized in terms of a Presidential *center*, gradually shading outwards, by degrees of remoteness, from Presidential involvement to *periphery* agencies. To paraphrase Miles's law—"What you see depends upon which way you face"—for those at the periphery may face in toward the center, *or* turn their backs upon it. In such a "dual economy," there can be an exchange of influence between center and periphery, or each can try to maximize its autonomy.

The search for political objectives must start at the White House, because the President is the legitimate director of this branch of government. Organizationally the most important points to note about the White House are negative.

1. The President's objectives are not identical to those of his Administration, for neither in law nor in politics is the President the

head of an integrated executive. The President's title as Chief Executive is misleading; there is very little that he can or does execute—and unlike a truly imperial magistrate, he never executes any person. The work of the executive branch is carried out by operating departments granted specific powers and responsibilities by Act of Congress, and not by Presidential delegation.

2. The President does not have the authority to issue directives to operating departments, and expect them to be followed without question. A Cabinet Secretary, by virtue of his office, sees problems different from the President. He is aware of the interests of departmental clients, and of their allies in Congress. Moreover, each department head, while appointed by the President, must be confirmed by the Senate. The annual appropriation process subjects each department to continuing Congressional oversight. The lesser political status of a Cabinet Secretary will make him less able to resist pressures from outside the executive branch—and this external vulnerability may make him hesitate or unwilling to do all that the President wants him to do.

3. The President lacks the organizational resources to direct the federal executive. The Executive Office of the President is meant to manage the President's business, and not the work of the whole executive branch. It consists of advisers rather than of men with "hands-on" control of the bulk of government activities, which rests with officials in operating agencies at many organizational removes from the White House. Budget examiners, the Executive Office staff most closely in continuing contact with executive actions of operating agencies, remain overseers. Moreover, the relative closeness of budget examiners to operating agencies is purchased at the price of relative remoteness from the President. The few hundred feet between the modern tower of the New Executive Office building at the north-east corner of 17th and Pennsylvania and the traditional-style West Wing of the White House at 16th and Pennsylvania spans a great distance, when measured in terms of an organization chart rather than footsteps.

4. The President does not have the staff to ensure that his objectives are followed throughout the executive branch. A President can grant frequent and continuing access to the Oval Office to a dozen people at most. (As one veteran occupant of the Old Executive Office Building commented in an interview, "A lot of people I know spend a lot of time thinking up ways to sound as if they see the President a lot more than they actually do.") Personal contact is necessary, because only in this way can the President be sure that his staff knows what his objectives are at any given time. The growth of White House staff in the past decade reflects the President's desire to

increase his influence by augmenting his assistants. But such growth presents a threat to the President. There is always the temptation for White House staff to go into business for themselves. In the picturesque phrase of Budget Bureau veteran Roger Jones: "Now there are too many people in the White House who are trying to bite you with the President's teeth." (Havemann, 1973: 1592) The more this is attempted, the quicker the word gets around Washington that the White House telephone exchange is used by a lot of people whose bite is infirm, however loud their bark, because they are speaking with false teeth.

In positive terms, the President's job is best described as that of Chief Decision Maker in the executive branch. The thing that makes the President different from everyone else who works for him is not his superior information, intelligence, or manners. It is that he is the only man who can take the responsibility for the chief decisions of his Administration. Decisions are choices, more or less clearly stated, among alternative objectives and goals.

The decisions that a President takes are of two very different types. One type determines what government does. The words of the President not only state an objective, but also commit public officials to action. The decisions that the President makes in his role as Commander-in-Chief are of this type, e.g., the movement of troops to Korea in 1950, or military actions in the first and second Cuban crisis. At a minimum, the decisions must specify actions that constitute inputs to a diplomatic or a domestic crisis (e.g., the President's dispatch of soldiers to Little Rock in 1957). Usually, the President also makes clear his objective, whether capable of realization within days, as in the second Cuban missile crisis, or a remote long-term goal, e.g., world peace. Presidential decisions that commit the government to act are often risky, for in international affairs other heads of state reserve the right to respond as they choose. In domestic policy they are likely to be controversial, e.g., the seizure of steel mills by Truman. If they were not controversial, they would not require the President to make a political judgment.

The more common type of Presidential decision states what he thinks the government *ought* to do. The President states an objective, but his words do not commit the government to action. The "decisions" embodied in the President's State of the Union message are not binding declarations of law or, as in the British government's annual announcement of legislation, a description of bills virtually certain to be law within twelve months. They are objects of Presidential desire. They commit the President to an effort to translate his wishes into government objectives. But they do not commit the Congress or the Courts to accept his judgment about what government should do. To realize his objectives, the President must convince others in Congress, the executive branch, and sometimes state and local government that his views ought to become law. Only after he has succeeded in achieving his political objectives *inside* government can a President turn over to staff such as OMB management associates the task of tracking how his Administration is in fact acting to realize his objectives *outside* government.

The President's State of the Union message is not a calendar of bills that will become law, but rather a shopping list of bills that the President would like to see enacted. The actual legislative record of the year is the result of the interaction of decisions taken by the departments, the White House, and Congress. Moreover, the specific legislative measures that constitute the President's chief statement of objectives for the year are usually not initiated by the President. As Nelson Polsby (1969: 65) argues:

> *Where do innovations in policy come from* before *the President initiates them? Old Washington hands know the answer. There is very little new under the sun. A great many newly enacted policies have been around in the air for quite a while. . . . There is often a hiatus of years—sometimes decades—between the first proposal of a policy innovation and its appearance as a Presidential initiative—much less as a law.*

Chamberlain's (1946) study of major legislation in the era before the activist Presidency documents the role of Congress in putting many proposals into circulation in Washington before the President. Studies of the contemporary Congress confirm its continuing role in first spotlighting proposals. (See Johannes, 1974; Arnold and Roos, 1974) Within the executive branch, the departments have historically been the primary source of the President's legislative recommendations. Within the departments, bureau chiefs have taken the initiative, with political oversight for most measures usually exercised by an assistant secretary or general counsel, rather than the Secretary. In the Eisenhower era Republicans found that while the voice of the State of the Union message was that of their President, the hand that wrote the details was often that of a holdover bureaucrat from Democratic years, for Eisenhower's major State of the Union message "mixed with rethinking from on high a good deal of educating from below." (Neustadt, 1954: 566. See also Thomas and Wolman, 1969; Wolman, 1971: 81ff; Harper, 1974: 24) After reviewing central legislative clearance, Robert Gilmour (1971: 152ff) concluded that 80 to 90 per cent of bills continue to well up from the agencies and bureaus. Measures initiated by the White House may constitute the most visible portion of a State of the Union message, but Congress retains the power to decide whether a Presidential recommendation is enacted into law. In legislation, it is Acts of Congress that are binding, rather than statements of Presidential desires.

The federal government's budget is the result of the interaction of decisions taken by the departments, the Executive Office of the President, and the Congress. The President's first responsibility as manager of the economy is to decide what he wishes the total expenditure of the executive branch to be in the next fiscal year; in turn, this influences the state of the national economy, and indirectly, Presidential popularity. The extent to which budgetting personally involves the President depends upon his interest in the budget, and other demands upon his time. Presidents differ greatly in the personal attention they give to the Budget. Inevitably, the Office of Management and Budget must make the bulk of decisions affecting individual programs. In addition to voicing Presidentially expressed views, it responds to initiatives from departments which provide the documents that start the annual budget cycle. The cycle is completed by Congress. The Presidentially endorsed requests of departments are not authorized until Congress votes appropriations. Congressional interest in government objectives as reflected in the budget is detailed and intense. The President's veto power (and power of rescission) is a response to defeat on the Hill; it is hardly a positive direction of government resources.

At any given time, there is uncertainty about what the government's objectives are. Insofar as Budget and State of the Union messages incorporate proposals that will invariably be accepted by Congress (e.g., the "base" items in the Budget), then certainty is purchased at the price of stating noncontroversial and therefore, nonpolitical objectives. To be a political leader (that is, endorse proposals before they are consensual), a President must risk frustration and defeat in Congress. To endorse "no-risk" objectives is to turn Presidential power into a nullity, for it signifies to knowledgeable Washingtonians that the President is only prepared to endorse objectives after others have done the work of gaining commitment to them.

A President's enunciation of objectives in his Budget and State of the Union message commits him to work to turn aspirations into actions. A President must risk a portion of his finite supply of political capital in order to make a reputation. Even a man with the drive to initiate legislation of Lyndon Johnson was nonetheless cautious before announcing objectives. Before signing a Special Message to Congress endorsing legislation, Johnson required Joseph Califano to supply him with an assurance from the appropriate Committee chairman fixing the date for hearings to begin, a head count of how the committee would probably divide on the measure, an estimate of pressure group alignments, and a forecast of the news angles that the press would probably feature.

Success in promoting legislation in Congress increases a President's political capital in proportion to the risk involved. The greater the risk in a Presidential initiative, the greater the possible return or loss. To strive for far more than he might achieve is to devalue the currency of Presidential endorsement. Writers who concentrate attention exclusively upon the Presidency often suggest that the President is some sort of Superman, batting 1.000 on all his requests. Empirical studies of Congressional endorsement of Presidential proposals from 1948 to 1964 make the President appear a formidable hitter, but not a Superman.

Faced with a multitude of political issues, a President must take three decisions. First of all, he must decide *what* issues will be the topic of Presidential objectives and aspirations. Secondly, the President must decide *when*, if at all, he will intervene in the policy process. Thirdly, as and when the President decides to involve himself, he must decide *how* he should commit himself. Should he follow the cautious motto of being "ever stronger on the stronger side," or should he start with the intention of being decisive in the resolution of an issue?

The difficulties of deciding what to do are simplified for the President by the fact that there are some things that he *must* do; these activities take precedence over what he may do. As Neustadt notes (1960: 155):

> *A President's priorities are set not by the relative importance of a task, but by the relative necessity for him to do it. He deals first with the things that are required of him next. Deadlines rule his personal agenda. . . . The net result may be a far cry from the order of priorities that would appeal to scholars or to columnists—or to the President himself.*

The ceaseless activity of the President is not a sign that the President is directing events, but rather that he is being driven by them or running after them. According to Neustadt (1960: 156), "Trying to stop fires is what Presidents do first. It takes most of their time." The President is "the prisoner of first-things-first. And almost always, something else comes first."

The *imperative* concerns of the President—the issues that he must do something about—are of two sorts. The most important to the nation are those that involve the prerogatives of sovereignty: foreign policy, defense, law and order, and taxation and expenditure. These are the sine qua non responsibilities of government. If problems under these headings are not met, then government as we know it would cease to exist. (See Rose, 1974) As the head of the executive branch of government, the President is first of all responsible for maintaining the essentials of American sovereignty. To evade these responsibilities would be to default on his oath to defend the Constitution; to delegate them would make him a figurehead constitutional monarch. The executive branch officials most concerned with these issues—the Secretary of State, the Secretary of Defense, the Attorney General, the Secretary of the Treasury, plus the Director of the Budget—invariably constitute the President's "Inner Cabinet" (Cronin, 1970: 609). If they lose the President's confidence, then he uses staff within the Executive Office—e.g., a Special Assistant for National Security Affairs or the Chairman of the Council of Economic Advisors—to provide him with counsel and staff to deal with matters that are of central significance to him and to the government he heads.

The prerogative concerns making imperative claims for Presidential attention have a number of attributes in common. First of all, because they touch upon the continuance of government, whether immediately like a Cuban crisis, or continuously like tax revenues and appropriations, the President need not worry about whether to act, but rather about what to do. Secondly, the issues central to government tend to start at the White House and action can be directed from there. Only the President can exercise the powers of Commander-in-Chief. Only the President can negotiate as an equal with a foreign head of state. Only the President can transmit a budget message to Congress on behalf of the executive branch. And only the President can determine the policy of the executive branch vis-a-vis the courts, when significant constitutional issues arise. Thirdly, the President is much less dependent upon Congressional authority and upon the cooperation of state and local government, when imperative issues arise. Fourthly, the problems that must come to him usually involve little administrative "tail." The President's administrative staff at OMB and in the National Security Council is minute in size by comparison with such behemoths as Agriculture, Commerce, and HEW. If implementation is required through an operating agency, such as Defense or State, its head will be a Presidential Counsellor formally or informally so denominated. The President can draw upon him for advice and support through an operating agency. It should not be surprising that the resources of the President are sufficient to meet the defining problems of state, for they have confronted chief executives with far fewer resources than a contemporary President. They faced George Washington and James Madison, as well as Lyndon Johnson and Gerald Ford.

A second set of imperative concerns are temporarily pressing, that is, a Presidential response is required promptly, even though the substance of a problem may be slight, or ephemeral. There are action-forcing procedures that require the President to do something, e.g., he must sign a bill passed by Congress, submit a veto message to Congress, or subject it to a pocket veto. A second set of temporarily pressing concerns are determined by political exigencies that compel the President to act by making the costs of Presidential inaction very great, even infinite. (See Rose, 1972) For example, the Watergate crisis brought forth a whole series of events in which the President was forced to act, though it was not always to his benefit. The argument for Presidential action to bring benefits to the nation is future-oriented and inevitably hypothetical. But the argument that unless the President acts he will face dire political consequences can be immediately compelling. Demands to do something can concern inflation, unemployment, the oil shortage, or whatever is momentarily the cause of so much political dissatisfaction that a "do-nothing" response would be most costly of all to the President. A President would not be in default of his constitutional obligations if he refused to do anything about inflation. But he would default upon political expectations of what a President today should do.

When confronted with temporarily pressing issues, the President begins earning his salary, being forced to take on high-risk objectives with inadequate resources immediately at his command. In an ad hoc crisis, a President may be able to extract emergency powers from Congress or make innovative use of latent executive authority. If a pressing problem is continuing, then the President will have every incentive to farm out responsibility, by creating a new agency (e.g., the FEA, or the Kerner Riot Commission) so that he only becomes involved after the initial force of complaints hits someone outside the White House.

The strength of the President's resources when meeting prerogative concerns stands in sharp contrast to his lack of power when confronted with many temporarily pressing domestic problems. When testifying in Congress in favor of President Nixon's Reorganization Plan No. 2 (Committee on Government Operations, 1970: 41), Joseph Califano expressed the belief: "Our national security is no less threatened by our domestic crisis at home than it was during those earlier periods of international crisis." He went on to argue:

*Our President may need extraordinary powers to deal with our emergency domestic needs and problems. It is a shocking commentary on the greatest democracy in the history of mankind that the President's power to commit our nation to new wars and foreign alliances is greater than his power to rebuild cities, modernize schools or medical delivery systems or clean up the environment.*

What appeared to Califano, speaking from the perspective of the Great Society as "inverted national priorities of Alice-in-Wonderland proportions" might in a post-Watergate era appear as the enduring wisdom of the Founding Fathers. Some would even argue that the way to redress an imbalance would be to reduce the President's power in international affairs too.

The foregoing analysis of Presidential priorities about what to do is supported by empirical studies of the Presidency. From interviews with White House staff, Thomas Cronin concludes that 60 to 67 per cent of the time the President devotes to policy matters is concentrated upon foreign policy and defense; he describes domestic policy as "the orphan of Presidential attention" (Cronin, 1974: 234ff). In a study of State of the Union messages since 1946, John Kessel (1972) finds that the most frequently occurring topics are defense, economic management, and social benefits. Moreover, content analysis shows that the President most often uses the word "must" when discussing foreign affairs and economic concerns. In subsequent interviews with Domestic Council staff of President Nixon, Kessel (1975: 4ff) once again found these three issues of greatest concern. Wildavsky (1966: 231) also offers evidence reinforcing the case for priorities described above. Whereas the President's "batting average" with Congressional requests for domestic legislation was .402, at the same time he was hitting .635 with requests concerning foreign policy and .738 in defense.

All other political issues are *optional* concerns of the President. There is neither constitutional obligation nor intolerable political pressure forcing him to declare a Presidential objective. To describe program responsibilities of government in such fields as health, education, welfare, transportation, agriculture, or housing as "optional" concerns of the President does not mean that they are unimportant in the federal budget or to the American people. It simply indicates that the President can only attend to them after he has dealt with the imperative concerns of his office. If a President responds successfully in meeting imperative issues, he will have accumulated extra political capital to invest in domestic policies. Alternatively, he may claim that the press of imperative business prevents him from risking his support in "optional" domestic programs, for which he will have only a limited number of hours in any event. The need to conserve Presidential involvement has been aptly stated by Donald Rumsfeld, speaking from Gerald Ford's White House: "The President can't be the action officer on every problem in government. We are going to set policies and goals in this building, but we're not going to firefight every problem that comes along." (*Washington Post*, November 6, 1974)

The relative ease of Presidential response to prerogative concerns is made apparent by comparison with problems that the President may opt to take up or to ignore. First of all, the fact that the departments are clamoring for support may be a disincentive for Presidential action; they wish him to act for their benefit. Secondly, many optional issues cannot be resolved at a single point. For example, the handles to pull for effective action against poverty are not readily visible from 1600 Pennsylvania Avenue. Improvements are likely to require a mixture of public and private actions for which responsibility is dispersed among federal agencies, and also divided between federal, state, and local institutions. To follow through on actions, a President risks exhaustion in an endless effort to exercise power across separate political jurisdictions. Thirdly, the problems that the President can choose to ignore tend to be clustered in Outer Cabinet agencies that are "bottom heavy" administratively, where bureau chiefs have accumulated significant independence through the years, and close ties with client groups and Congressional subcommittees favoring objectives in conflict with those that the President would wish to endorse—if he chooses to say anything.

If a President decides to become involved in an issue, he must decide *when* to state his objective. A President can take the initiative in a matter, or he can hold off any public statement, until events provide a stimulus to which he responds.

One incentive for a President to take the initiative is that by doing so he may accomplish something during his Administration that would not otherwise have happened. A President who successfully states an objective and secures government action shows more power than one who responds to what is put before him. A second reason for initiating action is that a President may dislike the kinds of choices left to him if he waits until the policy process is so far along that he is confronted with unpalatable alternatives. For example, a President who remains detached from Congressional debate about an important bill may be forced to sign a bill he dislikes, or risk a veto. By initiating a legislative proposal, he can influence what Congress does, thus increasing the prospect that the bill Congress passes is a bill that he wants to sign and claim credit for as his own. In today's international climate, a President will seek diplomatic initiatives intended to prevent fires, as well as reacting to diplomatic explosions.

The incentives for a President to hold off action until forced to respond are very great when an issue is not imperative. As Dwight D. Eisenhower reputedly told his successor, "Every choice you make will be a hard one. Your staff will take care of the easy ones themselves." By waiting until an optional issue becomes pressing, the

President may find that he does not need to do anything at all. By delaying commitment to an issue until the need for a Presidential response is pressing, the man in the White House embroils himself in controversy only under pressure of events. For example, Presidents Eisenhower and Kennedy showed studied detachment from racial questions until the 1957 integration of Central High School, Little Rock, and a 1962 Birmingham church bombing forced each to register some response. Moreover, by waiting to respond until major disputants have taken up positions, the President gains a much clearer picture of the extent of support for alternative policies. If a President withholds public comment on a bill until it has passed both Houses of Congress and is ready for his signature, then he knows for certain that his endorsement will meet with the favor of a majority on the Hill. By contrast, if he initiates a legislative proposal, he will be far more uncertain about the extent and size of Congressional support.

After a President determines when to state his views, he faces a third question: *how* to state his objectives. Presidential rhetoric is far more flexible than the precise language of the statute books, or budget requests. A President can choose to advocate a specific action or he can state his position in nondirective terms.

The textbook picture of a decision maker portrays a man whose decisions are clearly stated in specific terms. In a large organization, it is particularly important that the man on top states clearly what he wants done, because otherwise his decisions will be distorted as they filter through layer after layer of subordinate staff. The President approaches the textbook picture of a decision maker when he is stating objectives that are the immediate basis for government action, for example, in foreign policy and defense. If diplomats are to negotiate or soldiers act in a crisis, then they must have a clear statement from the President of his objectives, or else their discretion will substitute for his intent. The Budget and the State of the Union messages constitute additional examples of the President declaring objectives. While the purpose of budget appropriations may at times be opaque, there is no doubt that the President advocates the appropriations stated therein. Similarly, in the State of the Union message, the President advocates objectives that are initially general, then specified in detail in a draft Administration bill.

A President will often state objectives in a nondirective manner. When a President is forced to respond to an issue in circumstances not of his choosing, instead of being clear, precise, and focussed upon results, a Presidential statement may be vague, indefinite, and uncertain in its implications. The President can, for instance, announce the appointment of a special adviser to symbolize White

House concern, or announce that the head of an operating agency is to be given the ambiguous honor of seeing what can be done about a problem. In such a case, the President's handshake of congratulation may simply be another way of saying goodbye to that concern. It is an invitation to others to take initiatives and state their objectives, while the President identifies potential support and opposition for alternative proposals. It also leaves the President free to accept, reject, or ignore the recommendations that he has invited.

President Nixon's first essay in identifying objectives—the report of the National Goals Research Staff—illustrates how very non-directive a White House activity can become. The body was established by Presidential decision in July, 1969 to consider the future problems facing the country. The Report described its findings "not as a listing of goals . . . or what our choices should be. Rather, it defines the questions, analyzes the debates and examines the alternative consequences." (National Goals Research Staff, 1970: 21) While the President had initially welcomed a seven-year forward look, he withheld endorsement from the Staff's nondirective report, fearing it would involve him in political controversy without compensating benefits.

In sum, there are five different ways in which a President can deal with imperative and temporarily pressing issues. At one extreme, he can initiate actions with specific objectives or, if he is more certain of the need for action than of the direction to head, toward vague and unspecified goals. At the other extreme, he may ignore imperative concerns, thereby defaulting upon his responsibilities in office. The frequency of crisis in foreign affairs ensures that often the President is responding to imperative events. Here again, he can choose to give a specific lead, or intentionally keep his objective vague, until events clarify. A prudent incumbent of the White House would usually approach imperative issues by taking a nondirective initiative, and then, after events had unfolded and support for policy options became clearer, respond with a specific statement of objectives appropriate to the problem at hand likely to secure majority support in Congress.

There are five different ways in which a President might deal with optional issues. The simplest alternative is to ignore them. The fact that the President treats an issue as "no business of mine" reduces its significance in Washington. But it does not decrease its significance in the eyes of those who hope to benefit from government action. A subject of optional concern to the President may be of imperative importance to an unemployed worker, a farmer, or a person in ill health. The President's refusal to give any direction to government is not evidence of disinterest in their well-being, but a sign that there is little he will do until other political groups generate enough heat to make it temporarily pressing. Then, the President may respond in a nondirective manner, if the subject is controversial and the outcome unclear, or with specific recommendations, if a political majority has crystallized. The number of optional issues for which the President takes an initiative, with or without specific direction, is limited by the time at his disposal and by his supply of political capital available for commitments where he is not obligated to run a risk.

The growing number of challenges to the survival and stability of American government, both at home and abroad, means that the minimum the President must do today is much greater than the maximum that any President did in the era between Abraham Lincoln and Woodrow Wilson. The frequency of issues touching the prerogatives of state demands a high minimum standard of Presidential performance. It does not follow, however, that the President's maximum powers have also risen. Modern technology has placed in the hands of contemporary American Presidents far greater .powers of destruction than those at the command of a Jefferson, a Jackson, or a Polk. But it has also placed in the hands of America's enemies similarly great powers threatening a President's initiatives. At home, a decade of unrest has demonstrated that novel forms and causes of protest have created challenges to law and order unknown in an earlier era. In economic matters, the President does not have sufficient powers to match the great additional responsibilities placed upon the White House by the expectations of the American people for material goods. The final years of Woodrow Wilson, the man who said that the President can "be as big a man as he can," illustrate the limitations upon Presidential achievement.

The maximum that the President can do has not risen in proportion to demands, for the President, like everyone else, is a man with a finite amount of time and political resources. The increase in demands for action in response to prerogative concerns has a high opportunity cost; it means that the President has less resources to invest elsewhere. The growth in the power of the President, a favorite theme of textbook authors and journalists, results from a rising minimum standard, and not from a heightened maximum achievement.

The easiest objectives for the President to pursue are those that can be sought by officials who are closest to him, that is, his own White House staff. He can, as it were, issue a declaration of independence from what looks like matters of lesser concern. By "drawing the wagons around him" a President can surround himself with persons whose position depends solely upon service to himself, and insulate himself from bearers of extraneous problems, demands, and other forms of trouble and bad news. For example, the White House has sufficient national security staff to carry out diplomatic negotiations with another nation when they are at crisis point. But the White House cannot monitor or manage diplomatic relations with more than one hundred countries. This task is pushed out to the Department (not the Secretary) of State. As and when one of the countries farmed out to the periphery presents a pressing concern, e.g., Cyprus in the 1974 crisis, then the issue is called in to the White House for a little while. The memoirs of the Viet Nam phase of the Johnson Administration (cf. Reedy, 1970), as well as the Watergate tapes, bear witness to the extent to which a President who has built a political career by sensitivity to the views of others can wall himself up in the White House.

The President's relationships with members of his Outer Cabinet —Agriculture, Commerce, HEW, HUD, Interior, Labor, and Transportation—exemplify the contrast between central and peripheral perspectives. In the first place, the things that interest Outer Cabinet secretaries are remote concerns of the White House. A President who jealously guards the time he allots to problems that are not imperative will have little time to spare for issues and objectives central to most Cabinet officers. These Cabinet Secretaries get the message quickly, because they find it difficult to arrange an appointment with the man who has named them to act on his behalf. When they do see him, they will usually be speaking as advocates of their department, rather than as Presidential counsellors, for if they do not put their department's view to the President, no one else will. There is thus a potential conflict of interest between Secretaries and the President.

The peripheral parts of the federal executive are best described by spatial rather than hierarchical metaphors. To the central staff trying to maintain contact with department heads and bureau chiefs, they may be "those bastards over there in the agencies." Those who work on the periphery—the whole range of non-Cabinet agencies from ACTION to the Veterans Administration as well as the majority of Cabinet posts—can view the President's declaration of independence from their concerns as an abdication of influence. It gives them the opportunity to pursue their own objectives, in whatever way they find best. What else can a man do if a senior official in the Old Executive Office Building says, "The President has his own concerns. It's up to each agency head to snake it on his own"?

Within a large government department, the Secretary is likely to find that his central post gives him a little of the eminence and a lot of the difficulties of the President. Operating powers are not in the

Office of the Secretary, but in bureaus and agencies. From the perspective of the White House, bureau chiefs and program managers are at the far horizon. The fact that most of these officials are (or until recently, were) civil servants makes them technically outside the pale of party politics. It also means that these men will have been in place before their Secretary came on board, and expect to remain there after he and his President have gone. They are the sitting tenants of executive authority—and possession is a good part of the law. They know intimately the context and history of every departmental activity and commitment. Program managers, men responsible for accomplishing activities, have their hands on the personnel and resources that constitute the outputs of government. An Administration's policy in a given area—if the policy is to be an achievement rather than a mere aspiration—must normally be carried out through their actions. Their very distance from the center of the federal executive is a source of power, for it places them *at the point of delivery*, where programs meet people and things in the world "out there."

At any one time, the objectives that concern a peripheral department will be more numerous as well as individually less significant than Presidential concerns. The MbO statements illustrate this. Departments monitoring departmental as well as Presidential objectives typically list four to ten times as many departmental objectives as there are those of White House interest. While MbO statements may seem of relatively little significance to a White House figure, they remain among the more significant concerns that program managers or bureau chiefs have in the year ahead. The fact that the MbO statements typically catalog departmental actions that require neither Congressional legislation nor appropriation means that they describe actions that program managers and bureau chiefs can take. By contrast, a State of the Union message expresses aspirations about what the government might do. Collectively, MbO statements may be closer to describing what the federal government is actually doing than a Presidential special message dependent upon the uncertainties of Congressional endorsement.

Program officials face questions different from the President's. The President or a Cabinet Secretary has a broad overview; his concern is with the creation of programs and their objectives. When responding to immediate problems such a politician is likely to think in terms of exigencies of choice: should we go this way or that? By contrast, the demands that face bureau officials are exigencies of performance: the things they can and cannot do are often chosen for them by Acts of Congress and by directives from above. Bureau officials may be engaged in reviewing, amending, or even subverting these rules, but they will also have the unique responsibility to make sure that the routine is managed satisfactorily. An agency that has the reputation for being administratively incompetent will inspire little confidence in its abilities to achieve new objectives. Putting first things first at the program manager's level means putting routine first. What the bureau does and how well it does it is the first thing that is noticed in any review of its operations. Questions about why it does what it is doing or whether it should do it at all are luxuries to be asked by economists with no responsibility for routine operations. It is not a question that many program managers can afford to ask very often.

It is best to think of the objectives of bureau chiefs and program managers as different from, rather than smaller or more numerous than Presidential objectives. One way in which they differ is in political significance. Bureaucrats can only act within the powers conferred upon them by statute and appropriations. Within such a framework, officials often enjoy the power to make discretionary decisions of considerable importance to those immediately affected. If their actions become controversial, however, bureaucrats wish to cite statutory authority for what they have done. Secondly, the objectives of the peripheral parts of government often involve high volume services, such as the provision of social security benefits to tens of millions of people, or of agricultural benefits to millions of farmers. Thirdly, the independent scope for agency action is often limited by its interdependence; for example, the significant discretionary decisions of HUD can only be made in agreement with other jurisdictions of government meant to receive federal grants. Because their objectives are complex and full of ramifications, bureau chiefs can be confident that the President will hesitate to become involved in defining their objectives. To do so would be to risk becoming bogged down in peripheral problems to the neglect of the President's central concerns.

Whereas Presidents and Presidential appointees are continually rediscovering the advantages and disadvantages of keeping remote from bureaus and programs, veterans of the bureaucracy know this already. They long ago learned to live without the spotlight of Presidential interest shining upon them. Their expectations of fame are less—but their expectations of autonomy are greater. Location at the periphery threatens them with political isolation unless they can mobilize political support somewhere. And the best places to look are outside the federal executive. Control of program resources draws them close to Congressional committees and client interest groups similarly concerned with the same program resources. Together, the bureau, the committee, and interest groups can form an *iron triangle*.

Political interest unites what institutions separate. In the many-splintered world of American politics, an alliance based in three different parts of the political system is a source of strength, not weakness. It gives bureaus privileged access to Congressional quarters where decisions central *to them* are made, as well as to such electoral support and lobbying as client groups can mobilize. The harder White House staff push against the iron triangle, trying to alter the programs it guards, the stronger the edifice can become. Senior officials of successive Presidents all testify ruefully to this. (See e.g., Bundy, 1968: 37ff; Seidman, 1970: 76; Kessel, 1975 Ch. 3)

The differentiation of organizations within the federal executive does not lead to autarchy, in which each unit pursues its own course without regard to others. The President's powers of appointment and budget review give him ultimate sanctions to invoke, if he wishes, to try to bring errant agencies to heel. Nor does it lead to anarchy, for the President's position gives him the power to impose some order upon the actions of his administration, where he thinks it is most important and most propitious to do so in terms of his objectives. A President can accept the inconsistencies that occur during his term of office with the stoic statement that he does not wish to bother himself with them, while scooping up for his own attention the issues that he thinks most important. The President and the departments live too close to pretend ignorance of each other, and the annual political cycle forces them together more than once. If they do not relate to each other in hierarchical terms, how do they relate: through conflict, through cooperation, or both?

A conflict model implies a zero-sum game, in which the objectives of the executive branch are either defined by the White House, or else by the agencies. Since politics is about conflicting views of what government should do it is understandable that two-thirds of White House staff experience considerable conflict with agencies; incidentally, this is true of *all* staff concerned with domestic programs. (Cronin, 1970: 585ff) The causes are White House insensitivities and lack of bureaucratic knowledge, resistance from the department, and the sheer complexity and diversity of the executive branch. Richard Neustadt's analysis of the Presidency presupposes that "to a degree the needs of bureaucrats and Presidents are incompatible." (1963: 863f)

> *But neither as a document nor as a created precedent does the American Constitution give the President of the United States exclusive warrant to be "boss" of the executive establishment. It gives him but a warrant to contend for that position, agency by agency, as best he can. Congress and its committees have their warrants too; so do department heads and*

*bureau chiefs. And every bureaucrat swears his* own oath *to preserve and defend the Constitution.*

Don Price (1965: 248) captures the ambivalence of agency heads toward the White House when he claims, as a fundamental law of Washington life, "Every bureau or agency in the government wants either to be absolutely independent of everybody else or to be established in the Executive Office of the President."

The fragmentation of government is such that the losers in a struggle within the executive branch need not accept defeat there as final. An agency frustrated by the President in an effort to get his endorsement for an increased appropriation or new legislation can try, through iron triangle contacts, to have a measure introduced by Congressmen acting covertly on their behalf. A President, frustrated by the unresponsiveness of a federal agency to his wishes, may first show this discreetly, so that only the Washington cognoscenti notice a change in the pecking order of departments. He can take to public opinion, in an election campaign or between, his wish that agents of the federal government redirect their efforts more in accord with his own objectives. Actions taken from frustration can harm both sides. For example, a department loses money and a President is likely to lose popularity—on the Hill, and even in the country—if he regularly impounds Congressional appropriations.

Cooperation for mutual benefit is more usual in the relationship between center and periphery; the differences between these two parts of the executive branch give each assets that the other finds valuable. Agencies need the President to give them favorable decisions, e.g., in the Budget and State of the Union proposals, and support, both in Congress and from the public, so that they can make better progress toward their objectives. In turn, the President needs information about programs, advice about opportunities for Presidential initiative, and, not least, agency achievements that give specific and popular meaning to generalized Presidential objectives. In optimum conditions, each side wishes to cooperate with the other, because each reckons that it will jointly share the credit for what government does.

Cooperation is very evident in the President's State of the Union message. It is a composite of proposals derived from many sources. White House staff primarily play a filtering role, reacting to proposals coming in from the outside—and the agencies have a privileged channel for communicating ideas. William Carey (1969: 451), a former Assistant Director of the Bureau of the Budget, offers this explanation:

*The Presidency is weak in* policy *analysis. It stands perched on a bottom-heavy administrative and operational system consisting of departments and agencies equipped with resources, clienteles and historical baggage which continually threaten to out-think and outrun the tenuous policy management capabilities of the White House. In the main, the Presidency is in the retail business when it comes to policy formulation; it reacts, responds, modifies and tinkers with departmental policy and program thrusts.*

A positive response from the President is valuable to a department, for it gives their proposal a priority claim for attention in the current session of Congress, and commits the President to support their measure with his resources.

Cooperation between agencies and the White House is evident even in the adversary circumstances of budgeting. OMB takes the initiative by indicating how much money in aggregate each department is likely to be able to claim in the next fiscal year's budget. Each department then submits specific budget recommendations for OMB to review, in the light of Presidential program priorities, as well as in relation to quickly changing macroeconomic constraints that are important determinants of the total budget request, and thus, of the mark of individual departments. If a department does not like the final recommendation of the Director of OMB it can (except in the unusual circumstances of the Nixon White House) appeal the decision to the President. The determination of Presidential budget recommendations is the outcome of a lengthy bargaining process, in which departments defer to the President's need to set some limit to public expenditure, and the Executive Office defers to the likely support of the iron triangle for programs that might otherwise be candidates for cuts.

The President can also increase cooperation by mediating when quarrels break out between agencies in the executive branch. An agency that is getting the worst of an interagency conflict can appeal to the President as the chief officer of the federal executive to resolve disagreements—hopefully to their advantage. In effect, this is what happens in the final stage of the budget review, when a department wishes to dispute a decision by the Director of OMB. One researcher (Gilmour, 1971: 156) argues that the growth in distance between OMB officials and the White House has led to an increase in appeals to the White House, as agencies tend to regard OMB as just another federal agency, rather than an authentic spokesman for the President. The chief beneficiaries of appeals on routine items have been White House staff, such as John Ehrlichman, who have been brought in to resolve differences that all participants know would not be sufficiently important to merit appeal to the President.

When an appeal is pressed, the President may follow the Truman model, and act as judge. Alternatively, he may follow the Roosevelt model and "bounce the buck back" to the Secretaries concerned, if he fears losing more than he could gain by acting as a conciliator.

Cooperation is most likely to occur, though hardest to prove, through the "law of anticipated reactions." A department uncertain about which of two measures to put forward for Congressional action will try to anticipate which would be more attractive to the President of the day, and promote it for inclusion in a forthcoming State of the Union message. As departments are permanent, it can wait for another President—or the incumbent's mood to change—before putting forward its second bill. Similarly, a President wishing to create a record as an activist, rather than a do-nothing leader, will look to the departments in the hope that they can anticipate what measures might be timely and readily accomplished, and to Congress to see what measures might be politically appealing this year. If the departments can give him practicable legislation likely to be popular on the Hill, the President can make such a measure "his" objective, and claim credit for it as his own.

The difficulties of cooperation and the consequent uncertainty of outcome are major disincentives for either those at the center or the periphery to regard the executive branch as if it were a team in which everyone contributed equally to the same result, or even to regard it as a farm-club system, in which it was the common desire for every player to move from the bush league to the parent major league team. As often as not, persons involved in the policy process find it as easy to regard themselves as *apart from rather than a part of* the executive branch of government. While officials at operating levels may ignore or evade White House directives (see, e.g., Halperin, 1974 Chs. 13-15), the President can insulate himself by giving greater priority to what the government ought to do than to the management of the programs that constitute the stuff of what government does.

.   .   .

Political objectives are found in many places. The President, especially in his role as Commander-in-Chief, can state a few objectives that affect the whole society. Usually a part of the federal government affects a part of a society. The whole society never makes decisions, as it might if government were the perfect market of a market economist's Utopia, or the centralized allocator of a Socialist Utopia. Nor can politicians expect agreement that their actions are taken on behalf of a unitary public interest. There does not exist in America today a political group commanding the assent of everyone to objectives it puts forward in the public interest. In nations with free political institutions, politics is a debate about what the public interest is at a given time and place. The regimes that most assertively say they know what the will of the people is are usually those least willing to test such assertions through free competition by political parties at elections.

Ultimately, the search for government objectives is resolved by an individual researcher's own choice of perspective. The particular set of objectives that can be identified varies with the organization chosen to represent that high level abstraction "government." Objectives unrelated to organizations, like organizations without objectives, are of little value to governors or governed. The MbO system provides data about the objectives that immediately concern officials in one part of the executive branch, the bound volumes of Presidential Documents offer evidence of another set of objectives, and collections of Public Laws record the direction that Congress gives to government. Anyone, whether economist, political scientist, or journalist, who claims that there must be a single source of government objectives is viewing Washington from clouds of wishful thinking. Anyone who claims that because there is no central direction to government, there can be no direction to it is fighting a straw man of his own creation. Neither clouds nor straw provide much food for thought.

The objectives of government are a composite heap, rather than an economist's tidy preference schedule. Collectively, they constitute a mosaic of individual and group objectives, goals, and ideals. The total mosaic is the joint product of autonomous decisions, cooperation, and conflict among many within and without the executive branch. In any four-year Presidential term, the mosaic is altered in part. But most of the pieces represent commitments carried forward from earlier administrations by the force of their own inertia. The mosaic metaphor emphasizes that the changes brought about by the government of the day are not necessarily incremental changes. Incremental change occurs only when a given objective is marginally modified. It is best symbolized in a budget, where all changes involve increments or decrements of a single quantity: money. By contrast, each piece of a mosaic is independent of another. A President can state objectives that "add on" existing pieces in the pattern. But he can also introduce objectives that make their mark because they clash with surrounding parts. The objectives that most immediately concern the President, such as decisions affecting war and peace, involve the greatest potential fallout.

To argue whether the President's objectives are bigger than those that he leaves to the departments is mistaken; it is to attempt comparison in the absence of a common measure of what is important. The President's objectives are different from those of any other official in the executive branch, because he is himself responsible for decisions affecting the prerogative powers of the state. If he often gets these wrong (and many of his counterparts in other counties have done so), then the government itself ceases to exist. Yet after hearing for the hundredth time that the President is the most powerful man in the world because he can order thermonuclear destruction on a global scale, one is prompted to ask the irreverent question: "What does the President do when he is not dropping H bombs?" The short answer is that he is then reduced to the position of other members of the executive branch: he expresses aspirations about what the government ought to do, and works to make these aspirations the objectives or accomplishments of government.

In the American system, the objectives that collectively constitute the concerns of government are expected to be determined by elected officeholders. This is especially true of the most controversial (i.e., the most political) actions of government. Only elected officials can legitimately ask their fellow citizens to accept government decisions, like them or not. Contemporary Presidents have usually guarded jealously their claim to determine government objectives concerning prerogative issues. The decisions may be difficult or unpopular, but no matter. This is the job the President is elected to do.

The President must husband the use of his legitimate authority, to ensure his re-election or to maintain his current political standing in Washington. The bulk of departmental responsibilities are left to Cabinet officers. While the Secretary is a Presidential appointee, he is not a man elected to do the job he holds; he may even be a failed Presidential candidate, a defeated governor, or someone who has never himself stood the test of campaigning for popular approval. The heads of departments, particularly in the Outer Cabinet and the agencies, quickly learn that the President has very limited time for their concerns. If a Secretary is familiar with the work of his department, as is usually the case in Agriculture or Labor, he has long identified with standing departmental goals. If a stranger to its subject matter, a Secretary can either abandon efforts to steer his department, or else go native, that is, adopt the already established objectives of the bureaus that make up his department.

A saving grace of the American system of representative government is that default of political choice near the top is accompanied by the "sideways" insertion of politics. The uncertainty of guidance from above means that an established bureau chief must himself find political support for the programs that are his responsibility. Instead of looking upwards for objectives, he can turn sideways to Congressional committees and client interest groups for direction. The status of Congress as an elected body co-equal with the President gives Congressional declarations just as much political legitimacy as Presidential statements. A client interest group can claim to be more representative of persons (or corporations) immediately affected by a particular bill than a disinterested and distant White House official. A bureau chief who sails under the flag of the iron triangle is not a pirate. Instead, he is a ship's captain who has calculated that the pay and guns that Congress can furnish him are greater than what the President may marshall for or against his bureau. The conflict between the two elected branches of the federal government is often real, but the two institutions are not engaged in war against each other. Both claim to be fighting on the same side—that of the American people.

To invoke the American people as a group with a single will is to hide behind a symbol. Decades of research into public opinion, both before and after the re-emergence of social and ethnic pluralism, have demonstrated that there are very few issues about which there is virtual unanimity among the American people, or even among those who vote for the man elected President. Moreover, the most popular goals, such as peace and prosperity, are not meaningful directives for government programs, because they do not specify how to get there from here. When an effort is made to specify how, exactly, government can contribute to peace or prosperity, political controversy arises. For example, economic objectives involve choices about who shall bear the cost of economic deflation deemed necessary to achieve the long-term goal of improving the economy. The alternative to a controversial government decision is not consensus, but rather no decision at all.

Ultimately, an investigation of government objectives leads back to questions of political power: who speaks for government? In the 1950s, the fragmentation of power analyzed herein was hailed as the triumph of pluralism. In the 1960s, the same picture was described as the triumph of "special interests" and a denial of the will of all. But the experience of the past decade raises doubts about the desirability of Presidential efforts to govern in the name of all the people. The tragedy of Lyndon Johnson's second term showed that one of the most sensitive politicians of this generation could become committed to objectives that terribly divided the American people. The electoral debacle of George McGovern in 1972, like that of Barry Goldwater in 1964, showed that a Presidential candidate proclaiming himself a spokesman of the "real" America can lose rather than win votes. The doctrine of the Imperial Presidency met an appropriately Roman debacle in the Watergate. Under Gerald Ford, the objectives of government today remain a mosaic, altering slowly and sometimes significantly, in response to the movement of many hands.

To offer an evaluation of the results is to go well beyond questions of management science, or, for that matter empirical political science, and to return to questions of political philosophy that are at least as old as those that simultaneously confronted Rousseau and the authors of the Federalist papers. The author of this study believes that the Federalists, with their realistic acceptance of the fact that men—including Presidents—are not angels, built institutions of governance that, on balance, are better designed to accommodate the multiple and contradictory objectives of the American people today than any institutions that could be designed by an architect of authoritarian or democratic centralism.

# A List of Sources

ABERBACH, Joel D. and Bert A. ROCKMAN, 1974. "Clashing Beliefs within the Executive Branch: the Nixon Administration Bureaucracy" (Duplicated: American Political Science Association annual meeting).

ALLISON, G.T., 1971. *Essence of Decision: Explaining the Cuban Missile Crisis* (Boston: Little, Brown).

ANDERSON, Patrick, 1968. *The Presidents' Men* (Garden City, N.Y.: Doubleday).

ANSHEN, Melvin, 1966. *Program Budgeting* (Santa Barbara: Rand), quoted in Virginia Held, "PPBS Comes to Washington," *Public Interest* (Summer), 102-115.

ARNOLD, Peri E. and L.J. ROOS, 1974. "Toward a Theory of Congressional-Executive Relations," *Review of Politics*, XXXVI: 3.

ASH, Roy, 1973. "Good Management: a Prized Commodity," *Civil Service Journal*, XIV: 2.

BERNSTEIN, Carl and Bob WOODWARD, 1975. *All the President's Men* (New York: Warner Paperback edition).

BERNSTEIN, Marver, 1970. "The Presidency and Management Improvement," *Law and Contemporary Problems*, XXXV: 3.

BONAFEDE, Dom, 1973. "President Nixon's Executive Reorganization Plans Prompt Praise and Criticism," *National Journal Reports*, March 10.

———, 1974. "Staff is Organized to Ensure Accessibility to Ford," *National Journal Reports*, No. 52, December 28.

BRADY, Rodney H., 1973. "MbO Goes to Work in the Public Sector," *Harvard Business Review*, LI: 2 (March-April), 65-74.

BRAYBROOKE, D. and C.E. LINDBLOM, 1963. *A Strategy of Decision* (New York: Free Press).

BRYCE, James, 1888. *The American Commonwealth* (New York: G.P. Putnams).

BUDGET OF THE UNITED STATES GOVERNMENT, 1975. *Fiscal Year 1976* (Washington, D.C.: Government Printing Office).

BUNDY, McGeorge, 1968. *The Strength of Government* (Cambridge, Mass.: Harvard University Press).

BUREAU OF THE BUDGET, 1967. *Steering Group Evaluation: a Staff Summary* (Washington, D.C.: Unpublished Typescript).

CAREY, William D., 1967. "Roles of the Bureau of the Budget," *Science*, CLVI: April 14.

———, 1969. "Presidential Staffing in the Sixties and Seventies," *Public Administration Review*, XXIX: 5.

CHAMBERLAIN, L.H., 1946. "The President, Congress and Legislation," *Political Science Quarterly*, LXI: 1.

CHAPMAN, Brian, 1970. *Police State* (London: Macmillan).

CLARK, K.C. and L.J. LEGERE, editors, 1969. *The President and the Management of National Security* (New York: Praeger).

CLEVELAND, Harlan, 1972. *The Future Executive* (New York: Harper and Row).

COMMITTEE ON ADMINISTRATIVE MANAGEMENT, 1937. *Brownlow Committee Report* (Washington, D.C.: Government Printing Office).

COMMITTEE ON GOVERNMENT OPERATIONS, U.S. SENATE, 1970. *Sub-Committee Hearing on Executive Re-organization* (Washington, D.C.: Government Printing Office).

CORWIN, E.S., 1957. *The President: Office and Powers* (New York: University Press, 4th edition).

CRONIN, Thomas E., 1970. " 'Everybody Believes in Democracy until he gets to the White House'—An Analysis of White House-Departmental Relations," *Law and Contemporary Problems*, XXXV: 3.

——, 1974. "Presidents as Chief Executives" in Rexford G. Tugwell and Thomas E. Cronin, editors, *The Presidency Reappraised* (New York: Praeger).

——, 1974a. "An Agenda for Ford," *Commonweal*, September 6.

——, and Sanford D. GREENBERG, editors, 1969. *The Presidential Advisory System* (New York: Harper and Row).

CYERT, R.M., 1967. "Business Management," *International Encyclopedia of the Social Sciences* (New York: Macmillan and Free Press, 2nd edition).

DAHL, R.A., 1957. "The Concept of Power," *Behavioral Science*, II: July.

DAVID, Paul T., 1971. "Party Platforms as National Plans," *Public Administration Review*, XXXI: 3.

DAVIS, O., M.A.H. DEMPSTER and A. WILDAVSKY, 1966. "A Theory of the Budgetary Process," *American Political Science Review*, LX: 3.

DAWES, Charles G., 1923. *The First Year of the Budget of the United States* (New York: Harpers).

DESTLER, I.M., 1972. *Presidents, Bureaucrats and Foreign Policy* (Princeton: University Press, 1972).

EASTON, David, 1965. *A Framework for Political Analysis* (Englewood Cliffs, N.J.: Prentice-Hall).

FORTAS, Abe, 1973. "The Presidency as I have Seen It," in Emmet John Hughes, 1973.

FRI, Robert W., 1974. "How to Manage the Government for Results: the Rise of MbO," *Organizational Dynamics*, II: 4 (Spring), 19-33.

GILMOUR, Robert S., 1971. "Central Legislative Clearance: a Revised Perspective," *Public Administration Review*, XXXI: 2.

GINZBERG, Eli, and R.M. SOLOW, 1974. *The Great Society* (New York: Harper Torchbooks).

HALPERIN, Morton H., 1974. *Bureaucratic Politics and Foreign Policy* (Washington, D.C.: Brookings Institution).

HARPER, Edwin, 1974. Panelist, "Advising the President," *The Bureaucrat*, III: 1.

HARVARD BUSINESS SCHOOL, 1972. *Case Studies of MbO in HEW* (Two parts) (Cambridge, Mass.: Harvard Business School).

HAVEMANN, Joel, 1973. "OMB Begins Major Program to Identify and Attain Presidential Goals," *National Journal Reports*, No. 22, June 2, 783-793.

——, 1973. "OMB's 'Management by Objective' Produces Goals of Uneven Quality," *Ibid.*, No. 33, August 18, 1201-1210.

——, 1973. "Nixon Approves 144 Agency goals, OMB begins Program to Co-ordinate Policy," *Ibid.*, No. 46, November 17, 1703-1709.

——, 1974. "MbO nears Second Phase, Linking Goals to Budget Process," *National Journal Reports*, No. 17, April 27, 609-618.

——, 1974. "Call for Fresh Initiatives Produces Mostly Old Ideas," *Ibid.*, No. 25, June 22, 921-924.

——, 1974. "Ford Endorses 172 Goals of 'Management by Objective' Plan," *Ibid.*, No. 43, October 26, 1597-1605.

HEALTH, EDUCATION AND WELFARE, DEPARTMENT OF, 1969. *Toward a Social Report* (Washington, D.C.: Government Printing Office).

HECLO, Hugh, 1975. "OMB and the Presidency—the Problem of 'Neutral Competence'," *Public Interest*, No. 38 (Winter).

HEINEMAN COMMISSION, 1967. "The President and his Executive Office: Summary of Conclusions and Recommendations" (Washington, D.C.: Executive Office of the President, unpublished typescript).

HESS, Stephen, 1974. *The Presidential Campaign* (Washington, D.C.: Brookings Institution).

HIRSCHFIELD, Robert S., editor, 1973. *The Power of the Presidency* (Chicago: Aldine, 2nd edition).

HOOVER COMMISSION, 1949. *Report on General Management of the Executive Branch* (Washington, D.C.: Government Printing Office).

HUGHES, Emmet John, 1973. *The Living Presidency* (Baltimore: Penguin Books).

HYNEMAN, C.S., 1950. *Bureaucracy in a Democracy* (New York: Harpers).

JACKSON, Senator Henry M., editor, 1965. *The National Security Council: Jackson Subcommittee Papers on Policy-Making at the Presidential Level* (New York: Praeger).

JOHANNES, John R., 1974. "The President Proposes and Congress Disposes— But Not Always," *Review of Politics*, XXXVI: 3 (July).

JOHNSON, Lyndon B., 1964. "Comments on the Presidency," in Robert S. Hirschfield, editor, 1973.

KENNEDY, John F., 1962. "Mid-Term Television Conversation on the Presidency," in Robert S. Hirschfield, editor, 1973.

KESSEL, John, 1972. "The Parameters of Presidential Politics" (Duplicated: American Political Science Association annual meeting).

——, 1975. *The Domestic Presidency: Decision Making in the White House* (North Scituate, Mass.: Duxbury Press).

KRAINES, O., 1958. *Congress and the Challenge of Big Government* (New York: Bookman Associates).

LEVINSON, Harry, 1970. "Management by Whose Objectives?" *Harvard Business Review* (July-August).

LINDBLOM, C.E., 1965. *The Intelligence of Democracy* (New York: Free Press).

LYDEN, F.J. and E.G. MILLER, editors, 1972. *Planning-Programming-*

*Budgeting: a Systems Approach to Management* (Chicago: Rand McNally, 2nd edition).

McCONKEY, Dale D., 1972. "20 Ways to Kill Management by Objectives," *Management Review*, LXI: 10.

McKINSEY AND COMPANY, 1970. *Strengthening Program Planning, Budgeting and Management in the Federal Government* (Washington, D.C.: unpublished report to the office of Management and Budget).

MALEK, Frederic V., 1971. "Management Improvement in the Federal Government," *Business Horizons*, XIV: 4.

———, 1974. "Managing for Results in the Federal Government," *Business Horizons* (April), 1-6.

———, 1974a. "The Development of Public Executives—Neglect and Reform," *Public Administration Review* (May/June), 230-233.

MANSFIELD, Harvey C., 1970. "Reorganizing the Federal Executive Branch: the Limits of Institutionalization," *Law and Contemporary Problems*, XXV: 3.

MARIK, R. and T.S. McFEE, 1974. "The Management Conference: Key to HEW's MbO System," *The Bureaucrat*, II: 4.

MARX, Fritz Morstein, 1945. "The Bureau of the Budget: its Evolution and Present Role," *American Political Science Review*, XXXIX, Part One (August), Part Two (October).

MEREWITZ, L. and S.H. SOSNICK, 1971. *The Budget's New Clothes* (Chicago: Markham/Rand McNally).

MOHR, L.B., 1973. "The Concept of Organizational Goal," *American Political Science Review*, LXVII: 2.

MOSHER, F.C. and J.E. HARR, 1970. *Programming Systems and Foreign Affairs Leadership* (New York: Oxford University Press).

———, and O. POLAND, 1964. *The Costs of American Government* (New York: Dodd, Mead and Co.).

———, et al., 1974. *Watergate: Implications for Responsible Government* (New York: Basic Books).

MULLANEY, Thomas R., 1971. "OMB Pushes Plans to Improve Federal Management: Still no Miracles," *National Journal Reports*, No. 49, December 4.

NATHAN, Richard, 1975. *The Plot that Failed: Nixon and the Administrative Presidency* (New York: Wiley).

NATIONAL GOALS RESEARCH STAFF, 1970. *Toward Balanced Growth: Quantity with Quality* (Washington, D.C.: Government Printing Office).

NEUSTADT, Richard, E., 1954. "Presidency and Legislation—the Growth of Central Clearance," *American Political Science Review*, XLVIII: 43.

———, 1955. "Presidency and Legislation: Planning the President's Program," *American Political Science Review*, XLIX: 4.

———, 1960. *Presidential Power* (New York: Wiley, reprinted 1968 with "Afterword: JFK" added).

———, 1963. "Approaches to Staffing the Presidency—Notes on FDR and JFK," *American Political Science Review*, LVII: 4.

NISKANEN, William A., 1971. *Bureaucracy and Representative Government* (Chicago: Aldine).

OAKESHOTT, Michael, 1951. *Political Education* (Cambridge: Bowes and Bowes).

ODIORNE, George S., 1965. *Management by Objectives: a System of Managerial Leadership* (New York: Pitman).

OLSON, Mancur Jr., 1965. *The Logic of Collective Action* (Cambridge, Mass.: Harvard University Press).

OSTROM, Vincent, 1974. *The Intellectual Crisis in American Public Administration* (University, Alabama: University of Alabama Press, revised edition).

OTT, D.J. and A.F. OTT, 1969. "The Budget Process," reprinted in Lyden and Miller, 1972.

OXFORD ENGLISH DICTIONARY ON HISTORICAL PRINCIPLES, 1933. (Shorter version in two volumes) (Oxford: Clarendon Press, 2nd edition).

PEARSON, Norman M., 1943. "The Budget Bureau: from Routine Business to General Staff," *Public Administration Review*, IV: 126-149.

POLSBY, Nelson, 1969. "Policy Analysis and Congress," *Public Policy*, XVIII: 1 (Fall, 1969).

POMPER, Gerald, 1968. *Elections in America* (New York: Dodd, Mead).

PRESIDENTIAL CAMPAIGN ACTIVITIES OF 1972. *Select Committee on Watergate and Related Activities: Use of Incumbency—Responsive Program*, Book 19 (Washington, D.C.: Government Printing Office).

PRESSMAN, J.L. and A. WILDAVSKY, 1973. *Implementation* (Berkeley: University of California Press).

PRICE, Don K., 1965. "The Executive Office of the President," in Henry M. Jackson, 1965.

QUADE, E.S., 1966. "Systems Analysis Techniques for Planning—Programming—Budgeting," in F.J. Lyden and Ernest G. Miller, 1972.

REEDY, George, 1970. *The Twilight of the Presidency* (New York: Mentor).

ROCKEFELLER, Nelson, 1965. "The Executive Office of the President," in Henry M. Jackson, 1965.

ROSE, Richard, 1970. *People in Politics: Observations across the Atlantic* (New York: Basic Books).

——, 1972. "The Market for Policy Indicators," in Andrew Shonfield and Stella Shaw, editors, *Social Indicators and Social Policy* (London: Heinemann).

——, 1973. "Models of Governing," *Comparative Politics*, V: 4.

——, 1973a. "Comparing Public Policy," *European Journal of Political Research*, I: 1.

——, 1974. "On the Evolution of Public Policy in Western Nations" (Warsaw: Paper to Polish Academy of Sciences/Committee on Political Sociology Conference).

——, 1974a. "Housing Objectives and Policy Indicators" in Richard Rose, editor, *The Management of Urban Change in Britain and Germany* (Beverly Hills: Sage).

ROSSITER, Clinton, 1956. "The Presidency—Focus of Leadership," *The New York Times*, November 11.

SAFFELL, David C., editor, 1974. *Watergate: its Effects on the American Political System* (Cambridge, Mass.: Winthrop).

SCHICK, Allen, 1970. "The Budget Bureau that Was: Thoughts on the Rise, Decline and Future of a Presidential Agency," *Law and Contemporary Problems*, XXXV: 3.

SCHLESINGER, Arthur M., Jr., 1965. *A Thousand Days* (London: Andre Deutsch).

SEIDMAN, Harold, 1970. *Politics, Position and Power* (New York: Oxford University Press).

———, 1972. "Crisis of Confidence in Government," *Political Quarterly*, XLIII: 1.

SHELDON, Oliver, 1933. "Management," in *International Encyclopedia of the Social Sciences* (New York: Macmillan).

SMITH, Harold, 1945. *The Management of Your Government* (New York: McGraw-Hill).

SORENSEN, Theodore C., 1963. *Decision-Making in the White House* (New York: Columbia University, 1963).

STILLMAN, R.J., 1973. "Woodrow Wilson and the Study of Administration," *American Political Science Review*, LXVII: 2.

THOMAS, Norman, and Harold WOLMAN, 1969. "The Presidency and Policy Formulation: the Task Force Device," *Public Administration Review*, XXIX: 5.

UDALL, Morris K., 1972. *A Report on the Growth of the Executive Office of the President, 1955-1973* (Washington, D.C.: Government Printing Office for Committee on Post Office and Civil Service, House of Representatives).

WEBSTER'S SEVENTH NEW COLLEGIATE DICTIONARY, 1963. (Springfield, Mass.: G. and C. Merrian Co.).

WEISS, Carol, 1972. *Evaluation Research* (Englewood Cliffs, N.J.: Prentice-Hall).

WHOLEY, Joseph et al., 1974. "If You Don't Care Where You Get to, Then it Doesn't Matter Which Way you Go" (Dartmouth College: OECD Seminar on Social Research and Public Policies).

WILDAVSKY, Aaron, 1966. "The Two Presidencies," *Trans-Action*, IV: 2.

———, editor, 1969. *The Presidency* (Boston: Little, Brown).

———, 1974. *The Politics of the Budgetary Process* (Boston: Little, Brown, 2nd edition).

WOLL, Peter and Rochelle JONES, 1973. "Bureaucratic Defense in Depth," *The Nation*, September 17, reprinted in David C. Saffell, 1974.

WOLMAN, Harold, 1971. *Politics of Federal Housing* (New York: Dodd, Mead).

WOOD, Robert, 1970. "When Government Works," *The Public Interest*, No. 18 (Winter).

# Index